# CONFLICTS UNENDING

# Conflicts Unending

THE UNITED STATES AND

REGIONAL DISPUTES

## Richard N. Haass

YALE UNIVERSITY PRESS *New Haven & London*

Published with assistance from the foundation established in memory of Philip Hamilton McMillan of the Class of 1894, Yale College. Parts of this book first appeared in slightly different form in the following publications: *Survival* (May–June 1988), published by the International Institute for Strategic Studies; *Commentary* (August 1986), reprinted by permission, all rights reserved; *Washington Quarterly* (Spring 1987, Spring 1988), published by MIT Press, reprinted by permission, and *Orbis* (Fall 1986, Winter 1988).

Designed by Richard Hendel.
Set in Trump type
by Marathon Typography Service, Inc., Durham, NC.

Printed in the United States of America.

Library of Congress Cataloging-in-Publication Data
Haass, Richard.
 Conflicts unending : the United States and regional disputes / Richard N. Haass.
  p. cm.
 Includes bibliographical references.
  ISBN 0-300-04555-7 (alk. paper)
 1. United States—Foreign relations—1981- 2. World politics—1985-1995. 3. Pacific settlement of international disputes. I. Title.
  E881.H33 1990
  327.73—dc20 89-38200
   CIP

The paper in this book meets the guidelines for permanence and durability of the Committee on Production Guidelines for Book Longevity of the Council on Library Resources.

10 9 8 7 6 5 4 3 2 1

*To my parents*

EDGAR: *Away, old man, —give me thy hand, —away!*
*King Lear hath lost, he and his daughter ta'en:*
*Give me thy hand; come on.*

GLOSTER: *No further, sir; a man may rot even here.*

EDGAR: *What, in ill thoughts again? Men must endure*
*Their going hence, even as their coming hither:*
*Ripeness is all: —come on.*

GLOSTER: *And that's true too.*

*King Lear*
(act 5, scene 2)

# CONTENTS

# PREFACE

This book has been a long time coming—in the thinking stage, and in its writing, editing, and revision. It is difficult to say just how long a time it has been, for I did not set out to write this book or indeed any book on the subject of managing regional conflicts: one more or less evolved.

My interest in the subject dates back to my undergraduate years at Oberlin, when I first learned about the Arab-Israeli conflict. A year in Israel helped me gain a knowledge of the region, as did several subsequent visits to Israel and to many of the Arab countries. Especially valuable was my trip to the region in spring 1988, when I traveled as a member of the study group of the Washington Institute for Near East Policy.

Travel and study provided similar opportunities to learn about some of the other conflicts discussed in this book. While living for nearly six years in the United Kingdom during the 1970s (three in Oxford as a graduate student, and then several more in London at the International Institute for Strategic Studies), I gained some insight into the tragedy of Northern Ireland. My work on my doctoral thesis (on American policy toward Southwest Asia) and travel sponsored by the U.S. Information Agency introduced me to South Asia, and a trip made possible by the South Africa Foundation gave me my personal experience with South Africa.

Cyprus is a bit different. Although my initial introduction to the island (other than as a tourist) came in the fateful summer of 1974, when I first worked as a foreign affairs aide in the U.S. Senate, I had a chance to deal closely with Cyprus while serving

in the State Department in the early 1980s. For two years
(1983–85) I was the department's special Cyprus coordinator; the
post was created as an expression of American interest in the fate
of the island and as something to facilitate diplomacy. In that
capacity I met regularly with the secretary-general of the United
Nations and his senior staff, and with the president of Cyprus,
the Turkish Cypriot leader, and the senior leadership of both
Greece and Turkey. More than any other experience (until my
current one) this position gave me a feel for just why regional
conflicts can go on as they do despite the apparent logic and pull
of possible solutions.

I left the State Department in August 1985 to take up a teach-
ing position at Harvard University's John F. Kennedy School of
Government. Fortunately, the position left me a good deal of time
to read, think, and write. One project in particular—a book on
arms control that I wrote and edited with my close friend and
colleague Al Carnesale—made me reflect a good deal on the
preconditions for international agreements, albeit of a unique
sort. At the same time I was able to produce a number of articles
for various journals—*Commentary, Orbis, Washington Quarterly,
Survival*—that addressed a number of distinct regional conflicts
and what the United States should do about them. I think it was
after the third of these efforts that Dan Pipes, the editor of *Orbis*,
suggested that a strong thread ran through my writings, and that I
might want to consider fleshing out my ideas in a book. A grant
from the J. Howard Pew Freedom Trust and the Pew Initiative in
Diplomatic Training enabled me to pull some of my thoughts
together; what you see here is the final result.

This book is intended for the generalist as well as the special-
ist. My purpose, though, is not to write the definitive analysis of
any one conflict (much less its history), but to use all five conflicts
as case studies, to highlight a way of thinking about disputes and
what might be done about them when they resist solution. Such
an approach ought, at least in principle, to interest people regardless of how much they know of the conflict in question. Such an
approach ought also to be of value even as the specifics change,
as they inevitably will over time.

I should add that the book is aimed also at practitioners, or sometime practitioners like me. The book is the product of not a little frustration on my part, for with a few exceptions the writing and thinking on negotiations is too technical and narrow. Making matters worse, a good deal of the writing on specific conflicts is too far removed from political and operational constraints. This is an attempt to bridge the gaps.

Not surprisingly, I owe much to many people. I would like to begin with my former colleagues at the State Department, some of whom are also current colleagues. Here Rick Burt, Bob Blackwill, and Larry Eagleburger (among others) did much to educate me in the ways of bureaucracy and in what it takes to be effective. I also owe a tremendous debt to my associates at the Kennedy School. People such as Graham Allison, Al Carnesale, Dick Neustadt, Tom Schelling, Glenn Loury, and Joe Nye made lunch far more than a culinary experience, which in any case it often was not. Julia Marsh and Karen Barnette were lifesavers in helping to prepare the manuscript. And I want to acknowledge a special debt to Simon Serfaty, Barbara Johnson, Audrey Abraham, and the many others at the Johns Hopkins Foreign Policy Institute who made a space for me during the final stage of preparing this manuscript in late 1988.

Like any author, I want to thank those who read part or all of the manuscript during its many stages. Hans Binnendijk, William Quandt, Stanley Hoffmann, Sam Huntington, Dennis Ross, David Welch, Sandra Charles, David Passage, Carol Darr, Ronald Heifitz, Mark Moore, Eileen Babbitt, Fritz Mayer, Jim Sibenius, Peter Zimmerman, Arthur Applbaum, Aaron Miller, John Kelly, Dan Pipes, Jim Wilkinson, Louis Dunn, Kurt Campbell, Brad Roberts, Ray Seitz, Shirley Williams, Jennifer Booth, Liz Ondaatje, Sean Lynn-Jones, William Ury, I. William Zartman, Louis Kriesberg, Robert Myers, Ross Rodgers—all have earned my sincere appreciation. John Covell and Fred Kameny at Yale University Press have earned my eternal gratitude for their editing of the manuscript.

Last, I should point out that at time of publication I am on leave from the Kennedy School and back in government, as a special assistant to the president and the senior director for Near East and South Asian affairs on the staff of the National Security Council. Save for some editing and the addition of references to a few publicly known developments, the final manuscript was completed before I assumed my new responsibilities in January 1989. As a result, this book ought to be read as depicting my personal views only and not necessarily as reflecting the official policy of the U.S. government.

# INTRODUCTION

Conflict is the norm for international affairs. Ambition, ideology, greed, security, insecurity, miscalculation, accident, ignorance, hatred—these and other explanations of human behavior account for the prevalence of tension and at times war between nation-states. Eliminating the sources of conflict is rarely a realistic possibility; instead, Americans and other would-be peacemakers must often content themselves with managing the tensions so that situations do not deteriorate. Yet if conflict is the norm, it is no less true that states and those who rule them have demonstrated an ability to limit the intensity of their conflicts. Between or among rivals, not every disagreement leads to war; just as important, not every war leads to complete submission or annihilation of one of the participants.

The realistic alternative to conflict is diplomatic management. The term is employed here not in an organizational or business sense of arranging and getting the most out of available resources, but rather in the sense of "dealing with." Management is not solution, which implies the end of conflict through a meeting of minds engendered by compromise, but rather something very different. Frictions with friends, disputes with foes, rivalries involving various interests—in short, the stuff of international relations and foreign policy—are rarely amenable to solution and must be managed.

The reasons are several. Some disputes simply lack a potential resolution that would benefit both parties. They are all-or-nothing disputes, or, to use the term of contemporary political science, zero-sum games, in that what one party would achieve the other would sacrifice; the latter participant normally has little or no reason to reach agreement. In other situations, where apparently reasonable compromises can be formulated, political leaders are often unwilling or unable to risk the appearance of settling for half a loaf. The best that can reasonably be expected of diplomats in these cases is that they bring about some modest degree of progress or, failing that, at least keep things from getting worse. At the heart of management is an appreciation of the limits of foreign policy and the risks inherent in ignoring them.

This modesty may not sit well with everyone. Fundamental to the American approach to politics, domestic and foreign alike, is a belief in solutions. The idea that problems can be solved if only enough dedication and imagination are applied is pervasive and lies at the heart of American political culture. Americans often assume that a deal can always be struck, that people can somehow "get to yes," if only they are sufficiently reasonable, sensitive, patient, and accommodating. Compromise is seen as the essence of diplomacy.

It is not difficult to see the sources of this thinking. The United States is an Anglo-Saxon society with a strong legal tradition that prescribes norms and proscribes certain kinds of behavior. It is also a society with a strongly market-oriented economy, one that again emphasizes the possibility of reaching mutually beneficial arrangements. A mistrust of extremism may reflect too the fact that for the most part the United States has not been an ideological society. Growth and mobility have eased potential class-consciousness and frictions. The system allows the individual latitude and opportunity; there is for this reason little attraction to philosophies that reject or seek to destroy the system. Most Americans subscribe to the notion that there are few problems either so permanent or so complex that men and women of good will and intention cannot sit down and resolve them.

American history also accounts for this innate optimism. History, to the extent it is studied at all, is seen mostly as a positive experience. There is a sense of progress and accomplishment, of wars won, frontiers extended, living standards raised. Man has more often than not mastered technology. Perhaps most important, since the Civil War no war has been fought on American soil; as one historian has observed, "what explains Americans most of all is that which they have *not* experienced" (italics in original).[1] Ours is a past not painful.

This faith in agreement and solutions reflects more than a legal bias and an embrace of a moderation that permits empathy and compromise. It is also that we are uncomfortable with ambiguity, and impatient with disagreements that cannot be ended by whatever means. This is not a phenomenon limited to foreign affairs: to the contrary, as Thomas Sowell has demonstrated, a dominant theme of American political thought and action is a belief in the possibility of reaching solutions that benefit all the parties concerned.[2]

Yet it can be argued that such frustration with ambiguity and unresolvable conflicts can lead to policies at best futile and at worst dangerous and counterproductive. Management in this circumstance often calls for an attempt to regulate competition so that it neither engulfs those who take part in it nor forces the United States to take steps that would alienate one or both parties. This will not be enough for some. But my thesis is that it should be: that those who would do more might accomplish less, that those who set out to do less may in fact accomplish more.

This thesis applies to areas ranging from arms reduction to labor negotiations, but it applies particularly well to various rivalries around the world that complicate American relations with each side and have the potential to erupt in war. Regional disputes are a focus deserving of attention. They are the most common kind of international conflict, they are inherently destructive and costly, and they are dangerous in that many could easily escalate to confrontations involving the great powers.

In light of these considerable stakes, many individuals in and out of government understandably maintain that the United States must employ all its resources, diplomatic and otherwise, to resolve regional conflicts before they get worse. But careful analysis suggests that a good number of them are inevitable or at least not particularly susceptible of negotiation or resolution. What should the United States do in such circumstances? As a rule the United States would be wise to lower its sights and work to build confidence between the parties, so that with time more ambitious diplomacy might succeed and in the meantime conflict not erupt. The argument is that by trying to do too much, by trying to solve what cannot be solved, the United States might lessen the possibility that progress will be realized or catastrophe avoided.

A useful parallel can be drawn to the field of medicine. In the words of Joseph A. Califano, Jr., former secretary of health, education and welfare, "Right now, when a physician is uncertain about the value of a medical procedure, his attitude tends to be: unless it has been proved ineffective, try it. Patients in discomfort tend to agree. In a medical system in which doctors are paid only for doing *something*, and patients want something done, uncertainty over diagnosis and treatment makes for all kinds of unnecessary tests and treatments" (italics in original).[3] Califano goes on to say, "I suggest we adopt a different attitude: unless the procedure has been proved effective, don't use it." What motivates this attitude is not simply opposition to wasting limited resources, but also the view that too much of the time treatment designed to improve the patient's health actually detracts from it. Iatrogenic, or treatment-induced, illness has analogies outside the world of medicine. One can find many examples in diplomacy where too much attention and effort not only frittered away valuable resources but actually set back the prospects for avoiding conflict.

That is the theme of this book. In successive chapters I examine five regional disputes: those between Israel on the one hand and the Palestinian Arabs and Arab states on the other, and between Greece and Turkey, India and Pakistan, South African whites and blacks, and Catholics and Protestants in Northern Ireland. To facilitate comparison and the development of common themes, each case study includes some necessary background to the dispute, a survey of possible solutions, an assessment of why solutions remain beyond reach, and recommendations for what the United States and other parties interested in promoting reconciliation can do instead of pressing for negotiations almost certain to fail.

Each situation poses the difficult challenge to the United States of trying to moderate rivalry while cultivating friendly relations with both sides and their sponsors; all five are commonly cited as candidates for major diplomatic undertakings. It is not apparent, however, that any qualify. To explain why this is the case, the first chapter is devoted to the process of negotiation itself, to the question of why some attempts at negotiation succeed while others do not, and to the question of what the United States should do when negotiations fail.

# 1

## THINKING ABOUT

## NEGOTIATIONS

Why did the Middle East conflict of October 1973 set the stage for the Camp David accords after the Middle East conflicts of 1948 and 1967 led to no compromise? Why did the Cyprus conflict of 1974, as well as the many diplomatic initiatives since, fail to bring about a successful negotiating outcome? Why did one diplomatic initiative involving Argentina succeed (the Beagle Channel episode) and another fail (surrounding the Falklands/Malvinas)? Why was diplomacy able to solve one southern Africa conflict (in Rhodesia/Zimbabwe) and possibly another (over Namibia and Angola) but not South Africa's internal division? Why did settlements to the Afghan conflict, the Iran-Iraq War, and possibly the Cambodian conflict materialize in 1988 but not before? Why do India and Pakistan appear unable to settle the differences that are prompting each to develop a capability to build nuclear weapons? What continues to feed the violence between Northern Ireland's Catholics and Protestants? Why have Central American peace initiatives failed for so long?

The answers to these and similar questions lie in a single word: ripeness. The notion of ripeness is central to international affairs. What is meant by ripeness is the existence of the prerequisites for diplomatic progress, that is, circumstances conducive for negotiated progress or even solution. Such prerequisites include characteristics of the parties to a dispute, some things about the relationship between or among the parties, and the nature of the dispute itself. These characteristics can be identified; if my thinking is correct, they should be present in successful negotiations and absent in unsuccessful ones.

The importance of ripeness ought to be apparent. As an analytic tool it helps to explain why agreements can be reached in certain situations but not in others. As a prescriptive tool it is perhaps more important, for it can help busy policymakers to identify disputes amenable to negotiation, or, in the case of apparent stalemates, factors requiring change and attention before diplomacy can prosper. But despite its significance, ripeness is often ignored by analysts and practitioners alike. It has received some useful attention,[1] but a good deal of what now constitutes mainstream writing on negotiation deals almost exclusively with technical considerations. The role of mediators and other third parties and the various approaches available to them are a common subject of study, as are the benefits and risks of bluffing, lying, and excessive arguing.[2] So too are notions of nondistributive (mutually profitable) outcomes, where all parties to a dispute derive equal benefit (or detriment), and distributive outcomes, where they do not (in the classic zero-sum case, one party benefits at the expense of the other).[3] There is also some valuable writing about the particular style of negotiations favored by those of one cultural background or another.[4] What distinguishes this school of thought is its involvement with the negotiating process and its preoccupation with technique, style, and approach. A second focus for much writing on international disputes, less the province of specialists in negotiation than of experts on the problems or areas themselves, is that of conflict resolution. There is a vast literature on plans that would solve at least in part the problems of the Middle East, Cyprus, South Africa, and Northern Ireland. What tends to be common to this body of thought is its emphasis on suggesting formulas that if adopted by the relevant parties would go a long ways toward eliminating the ground for disagreement.

Yet despite these valuable intellectual contributions and the efforts of mediators, a large number of disputes have resisted and in some cases continue to resist successful ministration. It is not because the parties are insufficiently intelligent or because the experts are unable to produce fair outcomes that would benefit all parties and improve the current state of affairs. To the contrary, advice on how to solve the problems of the Middle East or Cyprus or any number of other areas is available and worthy of attention; there are simply other factors at work that must be taken into account. Contemporary writing on negotiations suffers from too great a focus on the negotiations themselves, on their form and content, and from not enough of a focus on the larger context in which they are conducted. Except in those situations where one party is sufficiently strong to impose its preferences on others, it is ripeness more than anything else that plays a decisive role in negotiating regional disputes.

## Successful Outcomes

A number of negotiating successes of the last decade —the Camp David accords; the settlement of the Beagle Channel dispute; the Lancaster House negotiations over Rhodesia/Zimbabwe; and negotiations over Afghanistan, the Iran-Iraq War, and quite possibly Namibia and Angola—possess common features beyond the presence of skilled, highly active mediators and of formulas that met some main requirements of the principal parties. The significance of these features is underlined when one realizes that several failures of negotiation—in Cyprus, the Aegean, Northern Ireland, the Falklands/Malvinas, Lebanon, Central America—did not lack talented third-party negotiators or (with the possible exception of Lebanon) reasonable frameworks for solution.

Camp David is important in this context, for it is often misunderstood. Frequently cited as a model of what diplomacy can accomplish, it is in many ways a classic negotiation, one in which two long-standing antagonists were brought together by an active mediator to settle their differences. President Jimmy Carter played an essential role, and a package was devised that gave each side what it wanted. Israel sought to establish the precedent of peace with an important Arab state and remove the possibility of another major war fought on several fronts; Egypt wanted to regain lost territory and with it access to oil reserves.

But these factors had existed in large part ever since the Middle East war of 1967. What made Camp David possible were things more basic. The Middle East war of 1973 provided a necessary backdrop: as was not the case in 1948 and 1967, Egypt did well enough in the fighting to bargain from a position of some psychological, political, and military strength, whereas Israel was sufficiently tested in the war's early stages that its confidence was somewhat shaken, and its interest greatly strengthened in doing what had to be done to remove Egypt from its list of Arab enemies. (It can be argued too that these same considerations were in large part responsible for the series of disengagement agreements involving Israel, Egypt, and Syria negotiated after the war of 1973.)[5] Moreover, "American leadership was certainly a necessary condition for the success of the negotiations, but it was not sufficient. The parties to the conflict had to be ready for agreement . . . Camp David formalized an existing reality: Egypt, under [President Anwar] Sadat's leadership, was not prepared to sacrifice its own national interests for the sake of the other Arabs."[6] And it was Sadat's good fortune that in Menachem Begin he faced an Israeli leader who was prepared to give back the Sinai and who had the political strength to see his commitment through.

Domestic politics also played a key part in the Beagle Channel dispute that for years kept tensions high between Argentina and Chile. At issue was part of the boundary between them and the sovereignty of several islands in the waterway. Again, there was no lack of mediators, and no shortage of reasonable solutions; the crisis began in earnest only after the Argentine government rejected the *laudo* (judgment) of May 1977 handed down by the International Court of Justice.[7]

The principal obstacle to an agreement was the irresponsibility of the Argentine political and military leadership—the same leadership that brought on itself the tragic folly of the Falklands war.

It is instructive that an agreement to solve the Beagle dispute (under the auspices of the Vatican) did not come before January 1984, after the Falklands war had changed Argentina's priorities and, more important, its leadership. The actual agreement ending the Beagle Channel dispute, signed in November 1984, provided for Chilean sovereignty over the key disputed islands in the channel.[8] Although it largely accorded with the laudo rejected years earlier by the Argentine government then in power, the treaty was overwhelmingly approved by the Argentine people and the Senate. In short, it was a treaty that could have been signed years earlier if the Argentine government had so desired.

A third negotiating success, the Lancaster House accords that settled the Rhodesian conflict, appears on the surface to resemble Camp David, in that a tireless and active third party operating in a secluded site managed to bridge the gap between two antagonists (the process has been described by one analyst as "dominant third party mediation").[9] Yet there is a telling difference: the strength and autonomy of both Sadat and Begin proved vital at Camp David, but it was the doubts and weaknesses of the rival camps that did so for the efforts of Britain's foreign minister, Peter Carrington.

The negotiation on Rhodesia was one between two sides, each consisting in turn of two principal groups. The Salisbury team was led by Bishop Abel Muzorewa (a moderate black Rhodesian) and by Rhodesia's former prime minister Ian Smith. Smith, the leader of white Rhodesians who in 1965 unilaterally declared independence, had scuttled earlier attempts at negotiating a settlement. The Victoria Falls conference of August 1975, Foreign Secretary James Callaghan's initiative of March 1976, Henry Kissinger's diplomatic efforts of April 1976, the "all parties" conference in Geneva of October 1976 (presided over by the United Kingdom's permanent representative to the United Nations, Ivor Richard), various Anglo-American schemes of 1977 and 1978—all failed, mostly because of Smith's refusal to contemplate majority (black) rule.

But by 1979 the situation had changed. The collapse of the

Portuguese empire in April 1974 emboldened black African revolutionaries and provided them with important new sanctuaries and support to conduct guerrilla war. Angola's independence in November 1975 led to an intensified armed struggle. International sanctions were ruining Rhodesia's economy, and votes in the U.S. Congress (supported by the Carter administration) made it clear that American sanctions would continue. Even South Africa, friendly to Rhodesia, had decided for its own reasons that it desired regional stability and that the time had arrived for a settlement of the Rhodesian problem. Smith reluctantly recognized the inevitability of majority rule by going along with the "internal settlement" of March 1978 that brought Muzorewa to office. Years of international isolation, economic hardship (brought on by sanctions and fighting), and guerrilla warfare with no end in sight forced Smith's hand; for him Muzorewa and the constitution were damage-limiting options under which the small and beleaguered white community could preserve as much privilege as possible.

But the settlement was not enough to satisfy the Commonwealth states, the Carter administration, or the other principal party to the dispute, the Patriotic Front, led jointly but uneasily by the rival insurgent leaders Joshua Nkomo and Robert Mugabe. The last hope of the Salisbury team, that Great Britain would support it, was dashed by Prime Minister Margaret Thatcher's apparent conversion to the general view that Muzorewa lacked legitimacy and would never gain international acceptance, despite the popular vote of spring 1979 endorsing the new Rhodesian constitution and his government. The Salisbury side therefore had limited ability to resist pressures, although it was sufficiently strong to negotiate for itself a number of relatively generous provisions in what became the final agreement.

Yet the Patriotic Front also lacked unity and confidence. Military victory on the battlefield remained a distant possibility. The neighboring states had grown weary of supporting them and were anxious that the guerrilla struggle come to an end. The Patriotic Front was worried that Thatcher's government might recognize

Muzorewa's regime. Nkomo and Mugabe were suspicious of one another, and each believed (as did for that matter Muzorewa) that if the question of the future leadership of Rhodesia-Zimbabwe were put fairly to the people he would win. No one, however, could be certain of this.

In the end it was this lack of confidence and strength on the part of the two camps that enabled Carrington to succeed where his many predecessors had failed. Neither side was sure it could sustain the struggle and prevail; neither side was sure it could hold out at the bargaining table and not be undercut by the British. The tightly organized and highly competent British team (supported at key moments by the United States) exploited these insecurities as well as tensions within the two delegations. The result was a major success for British diplomacy and a peaceful resolution to the Rhodesian conflict.

Another example worth examining in this vein is that of Afghanistan. The modern saga begins in April 1978, when the Communist party of Afghanistan (then led by Mohammed Noor Taraki) seized power in a bloody coup. Twenty months later, in December 1979, the Soviet Union engineered a second coup, killed the Afghan president they had months before placed in charge (Hafizullah Amin), and replaced him with yet another Afghan deemed sufficiently loyal (Babrak Karmal). In an attempt to bring under greater Soviet control this strategically located country (surrounded almost entirely by the Soviet Union, Iran, and Pakistan), 85,000 Red Army troops entered the country; the number of Soviet troops soon increased to 115,000 as the small, lightly armed, native Afghan resistance to Communist rule gained in strength.

In June 1982 began indirect talks sponsored by the United Nations between Pakistan (the base for most of the Afghan guerrillas and their conduit for military aid) and Afghanistan. Diplomatic efforts met with little success. The Soviet Union, confident that it could prevail on the battlefield, showed little inclination to support the efforts of the United Nations to end the fighting. At the same time Pakistan felt little pressure other than the weight of refugees, a responsibility more than offset by Western financial and military assistance. Last, neither the guerrillas themselves nor the United States (increasingly their principal patron) was willing to agree to any political settlement that provided for Soviet occupation of the country or dominion over it.

Things began to change in 1985. Mikhail Gorbachev became the Soviet leader; soon after, the Soviets increased the intensity of their military effort in Afghanistan in what turned out to be one last effort to pacify the country. This failed; the military situation deteriorated from 1986 as the quantity and quality increased of outside military support to the guerrillas (including the Stinger antiaircraft missiles supplied by the United States). Against a backdrop of growing human and financial costs of conducting a losing war that was unpopular at home and hurting the reputation of the Soviet Union with the Islamic countries, Moscow (with Gorbachev increasingly in control) began to search in earnest for political solutions.

Yet the Soviets were not alone in wanting an end to the war. Pakistan, strained by the more than three million Afghan refugees and increasingly tired of terrorist attacks sponsored by the Soviets within its borders, also sought a diplomatic solution to the problem. And so did the United States. Although there was some utility in bleeding the Soviet Union, the war was also costly financially to the United States (which sent several hundred million dollars a year to the *mujahedin*, or freedom fighters). There was also the risk that the fighting could spill over into Pakistan, a contingency that would place great strains on the ability of the United States to project military power in behalf of an ally. Above all, there was the chance to achieve a diplomatic success with the Soviets at the same time the United States would be establishing the important precedent of a Soviet failure and withdrawal.

The endgame came in early 1988. Gorbachev first ensured that his Afghan clients would not object—something not too difficult to achieve, for two years earlier the Soviets had replaced the more independent Babrak Karmal with another Afghan, Najibullah, seemingly more prepared to listen to Moscow. The Soviets compromised on an important point, ending their insistence that all outside support of the resistance stop as a precondition to their withdrawal. Pakistan meanwhile dropped its insistence that the existing Afghan government be disbanded and replaced by a new government that would include representatives of the resistance.

The deal itself was relatively simple. Signed in Geneva on April 14, 1988, nearly six years after the United Nations negotiations began, the accord called for the Soviets to cease occupying and interfering in Afghanistan in exchange for an end to Pakistan's support for the guerrillas. In addition, the agreement provided for the voluntary return of refugees and the withdrawal of all Soviet troops from Afghanistan by February 15, 1989, with half to go before August 15, 1988. The United States and the Soviet Union agreed formally to guarantee the accord and respect Afghanistan's nonaligned status, and agreed privately that either would be free to assist its Afghan allies during and after the nine-month withdrawal if the other did.[10]

The Afghan success offers several lessons. Progress came only after important parties concluded that they could not prevail on the battlefield and that the costs of continuing the conflict outweighed the costs of compromise. This situation did not come about by chance, but as a result of policies designed by the United States and Pakistan to promote an expensive stalemate on the ground. Diplomatic progress also required that there be leaders in the Soviet Union, the United States, and Pakistan able to convince their colleagues in government that there was no rational alternative to negotiation. At the same time, progress required that no Afghan leader in or out of government was strong enough to resist the pressure of his respective patron. And successful negotiation in turn required a commonly accepted mediator and a formula that while including something for everyone did not seek to solve every aspect of the problem. The "success" of Afghanistan did in fact lead to a civil war for ultimate control between the government and the mujahedin as well as among various resistance forces.

A second case study in southern Africa also merits scrutiny.

For more than a decade the United States, along with the other major Western powers, sought both to bring about the independence of Namibia (Southwest Africa) and to end the presence of around fifty thousand Cuban soldiers who had been stationed in neighboring Angola since the mid-1970s. South Africa proved the key to both objectives, for it controlled Namibia while at the same time it provided important support to UNITA (the National Union for the Total Independence of Angola), the guerrilla army led by Jonas Savimbi that lost out in the struggle for power after independence was achieved from Portugal, and that has since fought to dislodge the Angolan central government.

Accounting for the conflict were a number of factors. The Angolan central government, although eager for the civil war to end, was loath to ask its Cuban protectors to leave lest it find its survival threatened. South Africa, though wanting the Cubans out, was nonetheless reluctant to cut off UNITA and see the Marxist Angolan central government consolidate its authority. UNITA had little confidence in schemes promising a sharing of power within Angola, and the Angolan government had little desire to dilute its own authority to a significant degree.

The long impasse in Namibia can also be explained. Whites in the area were comfortable with the status quo, whereas the black majority was too weak militarily to impose its will and uninterested in settling for less. South Africa had no obvious incentive to grant Namibia its freedom, given the modest economic cost of sustaining its own position, the certain domestic political cost to the ruling National party of "selling out," the likelihood that groups hostile to South Africa would dominate an independent Namibia (notably SWAPO, the South-West African People's Organization), and the certainty that South Africa's international isolation (and sanctions) would continue or even mount regardless of what happened in Namibia, owing to the international opposition to its domestic policies.

It is possible to explain how diplomatic success apparently overcome these obstacles. The key participants—Angola, Cuba, and South Africa (which represents UNITA's interests as well)—

accepted the mediation of the United States and the central role of the assistant secretary of state for African affairs, Chester Crocker. After years of negotiations the three parties agreed in New York on July 13, 1988, to principles that would guide any settlement.[11] Chief among these are the removal of all Cuban troops from Angola and of all South African troops from Namibia (the latter number about 25,000), and the conduct of free and fair elections under the auspices of the United Nations as Namibia moved toward independence. A subsequent set of agreements, signed in New York on December 22, 1988, spelled out some of the details: a transition to Namibian independence beginning April 1, 1989, elections supervised by the United Nations to be held on November 1, 1989, and a phased pullout of South African forces from Namibia and Cuban forces from Angola, the latter to be completed by July 1, 1991. Left unanswered was the question of political arrangements within Angola itself and the related matter of external support for the UNITA insurgency on the one hand or the Angolan central government on the other.[12]

It is thus possible to account for this second apparent success in southern Africa. No side in the Angolan civil war possessed the strength to prevail on the battlefield. At least in principle, a political settlement offered results that continued fighting could not. The Angolan government wished to end a war that was costly to conduct and (owing to the Cuban presence) posed a barrier to the economic assistance from the United States and the West it so desperately needed. The South African government also wanted to see the conflict end, not only given its human, diplomatic, and economic costs, but also to halt Angolan support for guerrillas of the African National Congress, who used Angola to wage their war against South Africa's apartheid.

Agreement also came because of new calculations on the part of those from outside Africa. One important external party to the dispute, namely the Soviet Union, had an interest in bringing to a close an inconclusive and expensive conflict; another important external party, the United States, possessed a clear stake in reducing Cuban and, indirectly, Soviet influence in the region and in demonstrating the potential of American diplomacy. Even Cuba appeared to want to end a war that was increasingly unpopular at home. Last, the accord became possible because of its own limited scope. By choosing not to spell out Angola's political future, in particular the relationship between the central government and the insurgents, and what outsiders could do to assist either, diplomats sidestepped an issue that could well have proven impossible to settle and an obstacle to what could be agreed on.[13]

One can also examine through the prism of ripeness the Iran-Iraq War, one of the most costly anywhere since World War II. Amid mounting tensions between Iraq and Iran, largely a result of the latter's promotion of terrorism designed to undermine the regime in Baghdad, war broke out in September 1980 when Iraq launched an incursion into Iran. Initially Iraq held the upper hand, as it moved cautiously into Iran. By 1982, however, the Iraqi initiative stalled, and Iran took the offensive, in the process coming to control large portions of Iraqi territory. Later the pendulum again shifted, this time in Iraq's favor, which by mid-1988 had recovered most of its lost territory so that the two armies faced each other across boundaries not much different from those that existed at the war's outset.[14]

As the fighting continued so did diplomacy, largely under the aegis of the secretary-general of the United Nations. Iraq for the most part articulated modest goals, supporting a cease-fire, mutual withdrawal to international boundaries, and a negotiated end to hostilities. These principles were largely reflected in United Nations Security Council Resolution 598, passed in July 1987. The same principles also animated the efforts of the United Nations to bring the war to a close.[15]

Iran's diplomatic goals meanwhile were as ambitious as they were consistent: an admission of guilt and payment of massive reparations by Iraq, and the ouster of Iraq's president, Saddam Hussein. This ambitious Iranian agenda reflected the superiority on the ground that Iran enjoyed for much of the war; many observers (and apparently many in the Iranian leadership) thought an Iranian victory a real possibility. It may also have been a function of the war's utility to the leadership as a rallying point for popular support. The result was a marked absence of any disposition on the part of Iran to compromise.

Beginning in 1988, however, the government in Teheran began to show greater interest in ending the war. This change of heart became apparent in July, when Iran suddenly announced its willingness to accept UNSC 598 without reservation. The decision was not an easy one; Iran's leader, Ayatollah Ruhollah Khomeini, stated at the time that accepting what for years he had rejected "is more lethal to me than poison."[16]

Several factors are likely to account for the ayatollah's declaration. Most important were Iran's declining fortunes on the battlefield and the prospects for more of the same. There appears to be an inverse relationship between prospects on the battlefield and interest in negotiation, to the extent that negotiation involves compromise rather than imposed terms. What may have been a key factor in Iran's calculus was the growing diplomatic and military support by the United States and the West for Iraq. The Reagan administration's "Operation Staunch," designed to shut off the flow of arms to Iran, was succeeding, and the naval presence in the Persian Gulf of the United States and its allies was limiting Iran's ability to act against Iraq.

Also a factor was Iran's crumbling economy. As Khomeini himself stated, accepting the United Nations resolution, however distasteful, was "in the interest of the revolution and of the system"; it had become preferable to continuing the war. This was a decision that few Iranian leaders other than Khomeini could have made. It would likely have been far more difficult for his successors to reach the same decision had he died while the war was still raging: none is likely to have had the necessary authority or control.

## Lessons of Failure

Negotiating failures are at least as revealing as successes. Their contrast with successful cases (many of which were failures for a time) can yield important insights into why diplomacy sometimes fails and what can be done about it when it does. The war over the Falklands/Malvinas is one of recent history's most dramatic examples of negotiating failure. Negotiators failed twice: before the crisis of 1982, and during the crisis itself. Each phase holds useful lessons for those who would attempt a third round and for negotiations more generally.

The history of the Falklands/Malvinas before April 1982 is a classic example of diplomatic drift.[17] Nothing had come of episodic attempts to solve the issue of the islands' sovereignty by awarding them to either Britain or Argentina or by finding something in between (the ideas had ranged from transitional periods to shared or indeterminate sovereignty to "leasebacks"). Neither country was willing to compromise on this key point, and neither felt compelled to. Senior officials in the British government saw no need to compromise on sovereignty and run the political risk of alienating the "kelpers" (islanders) and their rabid parliamentary supporters; in the meantime they preferred endless negotiations with the Argentines, which London believed (wrongly, as it turned out) would satisfy Argentina and forestall anything more dramatic. Argentina meanwhile saw no need to settle for anything less than a quick and total award of sovereignty. The Argentine government could point to some historical and legal arguments to buttress its case, there were signs of waning British interest, and no fear existed that if push came to shove and force were used the British would respond in kind. The only thing the two governments appeared to share was a disinclination to compromise.

The Argentine invasion of the islands on April 2 transformed the situation. For the United States, an obscure set of islands suddenly posed a major dilemma: a defeat and alienation of Argentina could set back American interests throughout the Western hemisphere, whereas across the Atlantic nothing less was at stake than the fate of Prime Minister Thatcher's government and the future of Britain's relationship with the United States and the Western alliance.

In these volatile circumstances, made more unstable as Argentina sent reinforcements to the islands and the British fleet steamed toward the South Atlantic, Secretary of State Alexander Haig launched his ill-fated shuttle.[18] The thrust of the American proposals, which have often been detailed, was to put off the central issue of sovereignty; instead the United States proposed a package consisting of Argentine withdrawal and a stopping of the British fleet, some form of interim administration of the islands, and a timetable for negotiations. Left unclear was the ultimate sovereignty of the islands and what would happen if the two sides could not agree; for this reason none of Haig's proposals was ever accepted by Argentina. Prime Minister Thatcher also objected to his approach because it did not restore British rule or mention that the wishes of the local inhabitants would be paramount. Toward the end of his shuttle Haig succeeded in angering both countries: the Argentines saw the mission as an exercise to buy time for the British, who were moving military assets to the area (allegedly with American help); the British feared that the United States might force them to back down and accept something less than the status quo ante.

Failure cannot be explained by an absence of intelligent mediation, for Haig's team was quite imaginative. Nor was the absence of a formula the key, for formulas there were. Rather, the mission failed primarily because the two governments became prisoners of their own rhetoric and political constraints, and could not finesse the central issue of sovereignty and survive. Some issues are truly distributive, or zero-sum, in nature; when this happens, as it did in the case of the Falklands/Malvinas, traditional diplomacy and its implicit embrace of compromise often have nowhere to go.

One other lesson concerning the utility of active mediation deserves mention. It is possible to sympathize with the desire of the United States to avoid a showdown between two friends that could end up weakening both as well as its own relations with each. Yet although an important factor in Argentina's intransigence was the widespread belief in Buenos Aires that Britain would never fight (much less fight and win), Haig's shuttle was undermined by the diplomatic activism of the United States (and its inherent message that somehow Washington could use its influence in London to protect Argentina from the potentially adverse consequences of its actions). Similarly, the denials by the United States that it was providing military and intelligence support to Great Britain, denials made in the interest of strengthening the perception that Haig was an impartial mediator, again worked against the effort to convince the generals that their challenge could lead to a war they would lose. At the very least, it is interesting to contemplate what would have been the effect in Argentina had the United States eschewed active mediation and instead openly backed Great Britain from the outset.

Lebanon requires separate treatment as well. It turned out to be a major failure for American diplomacy and for diplomacy more generally. The critical question is whether failure in Lebanon was inevitable, or might have been avoided had the United States acted differently. Both questions raise the issue of whether it was a lack of ripeness in the situation or poor strategy and diplomacy that doomed the would-be peacemakers.[19] In fact it was both. Modern Lebanon is in large part the creation of France, which gained a mandate for the territory formerly occupied by the Ottomans in the wake of World War I. The Republic of Lebanon was born in 1926. From the outset Lebanon was a divided society, delicately balanced between Christians (mostly Maronite) oriented toward Europe and Muslims (increasingly Shiite) oriented toward the Arabs, with the former enjoying political primacy even though the latter were a majority. This arrangement was predicated on the fiction that the Christians enjoyed a numerical advantage, maintained by a national policy of holding no census. It was a fiction that nonetheless seemed acceptable, for Lebanon (independent as of 1946) remained stable and prosperous.

What upset Lebanon's equipoise was the larger situation in the Middle East, and in particular the Palestinian issue. After the Middle East war of 1967, Lebanon became home to an increasing number of Palestinians. The PLO's presence in Lebanon grew in size and strength after a showdown in September 1970, when forces loyal to King Hussein of Jordan defeated and expelled the PLO from Jordan in what was in effect a civil war for control of the country. Increasingly the PLO operated a state within a state in Lebanon, which became the venue of frequent military clashes between the PLO and Israel. In the process Lebanon itself became politicized, militarized, and divided along a host of confessional lines. These groups were distinguished not only by their diverging objectives for Lebanon but also by their ties to various external benefactors, ranging from Israel in the case of the Maronite Christians to Syria and other Arab states for Lebanon's Muslims and their Palestinian allies.[20]

The result (by 1975) was a violent but in the end inconclusive civil war, with Lebanon increasingly resembling a medieval kingdom of warring principalities and foreign forces. Nevertheless, the Israeli invasion of Lebanon in spring 1982, coupled with the military defeat and humiliation of both the PLO and the Syrian air force, created an opportunity, however small and fleeting, for a settlement leading to a withdrawal of all foreign forces and a reunified, independent government of Lebanon. But despite the evacuation of the PLO in late August 1982, which removed one complicating presence, Lebanon like Humpty-Dumpty could not be put back together again.

There are several reasons for this. American diplomacy can be faulted in part: the decision by the United States to arrange first an Israeli-Lebanese treaty rather than attempt a pact with the Syrians, or better yet a simultaneous arrangement with Israel, Syria, the PLO, and Lebanon, can be criticized for wasting the opportunity at hand. With every passing day Israel needed more from a treaty with Lebanon to justify its controversial invasion and occupation. Yet with Syria and the PLO recovering militarily and psychologically, thanks to time and Soviet aid, the increasingly shaky Lebanese government of Amin Gemayel (his brother Bashir was assassinated in mid-September) was too weak and insecure to follow Egypt's example and reach a separate peace with Israel (not to mention a generous peace). The simultaneous announcement by the United States of President Reagan's comprehensive Middle East plan of September 1, 1982—a proposal that the Israeli government of the time strongly opposed—only increased Israel's incentive to drag its heels on Lebanon so as not to clear the decks for a new round of Middle East diplomacy on the part of the United States.

Ignoring these warning signs, the Reagan administration decided to use force to buttress its diplomatic endeavors. Marines had been sent to Lebanon in summer 1982 to assist in the departure of the PLO, then returned weeks later after the Christian massacre of Palestinian men, women, and children in the refugee camps. The marines had no clear purpose beyond their simple presence, and soon became a target for various Muslim forces. In part to protect themselves and deter further attacks, in part to demonstrate resolve, the United States not only permitted the marines to return fire but augmented them with battleships and aircraft. By so doing, the United States became the most active of mediators: it became a virtual participant in Lebanon's war.

The American use of military force against Syrian and Moslem positions in Lebanon was in effect an attempt to create ripeness and impose an agreement; the hope was that Syria and its allies might be persuaded to reduce both their level of military activity and their opposition to the agreement of May 17, 1983, between Israel and Lebanon if faced by a determined American and Israeli show of force. The American attempt failed, militarily and politically. Israel was eager to withdraw, whereas Syria was prepared to hunker down and wait out the United States. In the United States, neither Congress nor the Department of Defense was prepared to fight a war in Lebanon. With reluctance matched only by speed, President Reagan decided to cut American losses and bring the marines back home.

When all is said and done, it is not at all clear that the opportunity for success ever existed. Lebanon's patchwork quilt of Christian and Muslim groups had unraveled; it is doubtful whether any diplomacy could have restored sufficient comity. The PLO's leadership had set up a country within a country and despite their evacuation wanted to return; Lebanon's armed forces were too weak and divided to prevent this. Syria was not about to give up its goal of establishing political primacy throughout Lebanon; Israel wanted a degree of security to its north that no Lebanese government could satisfy and still survive. Authority in Lebanon was (and may remain) too divided to bring about order through negotiations or indeed through anything else.

Another dispute that has thus far resisted diplomacy is that of Central America, and in particular Nicaragua. The immediate problem can be traced back to 1979, when the Frente Sandinista de Liberación Nacional (FSLN, or Sandinistas) succeeded in ousting the authoritarian regime of Anastasio Somoza. Satisfaction in the U.S. government was short-lived, however, as the Sandinistas quickly expelled more moderate elements, refused to allow significant political opposition or independent economic activity, and began to support guerrilla forces seeking to overthrow the government of neighboring El Salvador.

As a result, in 1981 the United States entered into negotiations with Nicaragua. A deal was put forward: the United States would resume economic aid and maintain normal political relations in exchange for the new government's terminating its support for insurgencies, limiting the Soviet and Cuban presence, and moderating its appetite for arms. The Sandinistas rejected the approach; in its aftermath, the United States proceeded to introduce political and economic sanctions and provide direct support to armed insurgents (the "contras," or Democratic Resistance) seeking to overthrow or drastically reform the Nicaraguan government.

As Nicaragua's civil war escalated and external powers increased their involvement, regional states put forth a series of formulas designed to bring peace: the "Contadora" initiative of January 1983, the Arias plan of February 1987, the "Esquipulas II" plan of August 1987, the "Tesoro Beach" plan of February 1989, the "Tela" accord of August 1989. These efforts stressed an end to Nicaragua's civil war—a cease-fire, internal democratization, amnesty, national reconciliation—and provisions for regional stability, including no support for insurgencies, limits on military capacity, and constraints on foreign military presence.

All five states of Central America have agreed to these plans, yet peace in Nicaragua and the region remains elusive. Although there is room for improving the plans—for example, in the area of verification—any possible shortcomings in the accords do not explain the failure of governments to implement what has been agreed to in principle. Nor is there a major problem with process, for at various times the Sandinistas have talked directly with the United States and with the contras, and there have been a host of negotiations involving leaders of Central American governments and one or another of their Latin neighbors.

Part of the problem stems from the leadership of the Sandinistas and their opponents. Although President Daniel Ortega of Nicaragua is clearly first among equals, he still must contend with the views of his comrades in the FSLN. Even if one does not accept the notion that at the top of the FSLN there are doves and hawks, or pragmatists and hard-liners, it is certain that there are differences resulting from personality and philosophy. This could affect Ortega's flexibility to negotiate and, just as important, his ability to honor an undertaking if developments seem to be working against the Sandinistas' interests.

If anything, the picture on the other side is far worse when viewed from a negotiating perspective. There are clear rivalries within the leadership of the contras, and tensions between battlefield commanders and negotiators. There is as well a gap between the militarized contras, largely externally based, and the more politically oriented, internally based opposition. Last, the internal opposition is itself split among fourteen political parties (according to one recent count) and various business, labor, geographic, and political interests and organizations. Thus no one has been in a position to speak authoritatively for the opposition, and, as has often been the case in Nicaragua's history, even to speak of an "opposition" as if it were a single entity obscures the real problem, which stems from its not being sufficiently unified to provide a meaningful alternative to the government.

These problems notwithstanding, what might be the principal obstacle to an accord is the absence of a conviction on either side that compromise and agreement are preferable to doing without an accord. For the contras the calculation is highly complex. Their weakness provides incentive to compromise—their ability to hold out and hold on is increasingly suspect—yet this same weakness undermines their bargaining position and makes any accord that is likely to be negotiated unattractive and unappealing from their vantage point. And to the extent that an agreement ends the military phase of the struggle for power in Nicaragua that began with Somoza's fall from power, the contras' leaders could find themselves at a disadvantage within the opposition, where traditional party, religious, and press figures may possess more strength than former guerrillas would.

The Sandinistas' calculus bears little resemblance to that of their rivals, although the result is not all that different. There is not much in Nicaraguan political tradition that suggests support for democracy and tolerance of a loyal, powerful opposition; there is even less tolerance in the more narrow political tradition that animates the FSLN. Despite their desire to improve their economic situation and put an end to the armed resistance, the Sandinistas evidence little interest in an accord that would require them to accept a degree of pluralism sufficiently great to threaten over the long term their continued political domination. This calculation promises to limit what could ever be expected in the way of compromise from the Sandinistas, and this is especially the case at present given the weakened state of the armed opposition: the contras' weakness diminishes for the government the costs of not agreeing to a settlement.

For these calculations to change and for a deal to come about, a number of conditions would have to be different. The Sandinistas would have to feel a greater need to compromise—because the contras became stronger militarily, or because of Soviet pressures, or because the Sandinistas decided that their struggling economy posed the greatest threat to the permanence of their revolution. Alternatively, a further diminution of the military and political strength of the Nicaraguan opposition would enable the Sandinistas to do all but impose their preferences. Similarly, after years of consolidating their position, the Sandinistas might conclude that they could institute a good deal of democracy and still prevail, thus giving them the best of all worlds: power with legitimacy. Whether the "Tela" accord of August 1989 will give them this remains to be seen.

## Ripeness: Four Prerequisites

There are four essentials of ripeness. All are relevant, and the absence of any one will pose an obstacle to successful negotiations. The most important is that there be a shared perception of the desirability of an accord. Parties must conclude that in the absence of an agreement time does not work in their favor, and that they will be worse off in absolute terms, in relative terms, or both.

Camp David proved possible when both Egypt and Israel saw advantages (not necessarily the same ones) in a bilateral accord. The Falklands war broke out after Great Britain and Argentina each concluded that no agreement that could be negotiated would meet its basic requirements and that even conflict was therefore preferable to compromise. The Afghan accord materialized only after the participants concluded that despite the accord's shortcomings the costs of continuing the war were too high and the prospects for military victory too dim. Much the same holds true for Iran and Iraq. No such consensus ever emerged in Lebanon; it is too soon to say whether one has finally come about in Central America.

Second, even if political leaders conclude that an accord is desirable, they must also be able to agree to it. They must either be sufficiently strong to permit compromise (because of popularity or force) or sufficiently weak that compromise cannot be avoided. It makes no difference whether leaders are strong or weak, but what there cannot be is a principal party that falls in between: not strong enough to compromise, but only strong enough to hang on.

A number of regional conflicts illustrate this principle. At Camp David, Sadat and Begin were sufficiently strong to reach agreement. At Lancaster House the various parties to the dispute over Rhodesia/Zimbabwe were too weak to hold out. The Argentine junta was too weak to compromise on either the Beagle Channel or the Falklands but strong enough to remain in power until the invasion of the Falklands led to a debacle. The British, meanwhile, were sufficiently strong to persist in their refusal to compromise on the matter of sovereignty; it is interesting to speculate on whether Haig's shuttle might have fared better had additional British ships been sunk and the Thatcher government come under severe pressure (as it surely would have) to cut its losses and get the best deal possible. Mikhail Gorbachev was strong enough to get the Soviet Union out of Afghanistan; perhaps only an Ayatollah Khomeini had the ability to end Iran's war with Iraq and still remain in power.

Third, short of situations of imposed peace such as those which followed World War II, there must be sufficient compromise on both sides to allow leaders to persuade their colleagues and citizens that the national interest was protected. Formulas or agreements that provide for this are not that difficult to come by, except when some contested issue is truly considered nonnegotiable by important parties. Other than in Lebanon, where the absence of a formula may in fact have precluded agreement, it is difficult to argue that any of the failures mentioned above was due to the lack of an agreement that most objective observers would have thought to be in the interest of all concerned (and surely better than the alternative).

Fourth, there must be a mutually acceptable approach or process. Parties can settle disputes themselves, through the mediating offices of some third party, or by resort to arbitration. Given that most parties need some assistance but are unwilling to accept arbitration, mediation is often a key to reaching accord. The United States at Camp David, the United Kingdom at Lancaster

House, the Vatican with the Beagle Channel—all contributed in ways that were necessary for success, although not sufficient for success.

The presence or absence or ripeness is therefore crucial. Where it exists, substantial negotiating progress is possible; where it does not, diplomats are fortunate if they can manage to prevent conflict. At the same time, the absence of ripeness can alert policymakers to the risk inherent in simply allowing a situation to drift. Such a circumstance often calls out for steps designed not to solve a dispute or even move it toward solution but simply to keep things from getting worse, and it offers the opportunity to bring about conditions that would make ambitious diplomacy possible. An absence of ripeness is not grounds for inaction. Unripe situations require careful attention and sustained effort, but of a different sort. If attempts to solve a dispute would prove futile or worse, attempts to regulate the competition to see that it does not erupt into conflict are called for. Here the policymaker has a wide range of so-called confidence-building measures to choose from. Many of the elements introduced into the Soviet-American relationship—a dispute that in effect can be only managed, not solved—are appropriate for other situations. They include procedures that lessen the chance of accidental conflict growing out of a political or military incident; arrangements that break down economic, social, and political barriers between communities or states; assistance that makes it easier for leaders and governments to "take risks for peace"; and public statements that can make it more difficult for leaders and governments not to run such risks. Again, the task is to prevent conflict from breaking out and to work toward the day when solution-oriented diplomacy can prosper.

In short, it is necessary to adopt a new way of thinking about diplomacy, one that goes beyond the narrow definition of diplomacy as negotiation to solve disputes. To refuse to do this is to condemn diplomacy in many instances to irrelevance, and to blind diplomats to the possibility of taking action that can keep things from getting worse so that one day they can get better. This more modest view of diplomacy may not sit well with everyone, but it ought to.

# 2

## THE MIDDLE EAST

Virtually everything that has been thought or said about the Middle East for nearly two decades has been informed by United Nations Security Council Resolution 242. This calls for the "establishment of a just and lasting peace in the Middle East," to be brought about by Israel exchanging some significant part of the territories it conquered in 1967 for acceptance and recognition by its neighbors. Implicit in American support for this "territory-for-peace" paradigm is the belief that the status quo, that is, a Middle East with Israel in possession of the West Bank, the Gaza Strip, and the Golan Heights, is not only unjust but inherently unstable in a manner threatening to American strategic, political, and economic interests in the region.

Perhaps more than any other part of the world, the Middle East contains the seeds of dangerous conflicts. The proliferation of conventional, chemical, and nuclear weapons to a number of states in the region raises the specter that future violence will be of a different kind and scale. There is as well the potential for confrontation between the superpowers, given the important interests of the United States and the Soviet Union; but, as is not the case in Europe, there are no clear rules of the road for regulating their competition. Also associated closely with the territory-for-peace paradigm is the notion that the United States is central to the peace process—that significant diplomatic progress in the region requires its diplomatic leadership. Many observers contend that the situation in the region will get worse if it does not get better, and that the only way for it to get better is for the

United States to broker peace actively between Israel and its Arab neighbors.[1]

It is in part for these reasons that over recent years there has been considerable interest on the part of the U.S. government in persuading King Hussein of Jordan to step forward on behalf of the Palestinians and negotiate directly with the Israelis (this is the so-called Jordanian option). Others have suggested the potential utility of bringing directly into the process Syria or the Soviet Union or the Palestine Liberation Organization (PLO), possibly by holding an international conference. What all such proposals have in common is the premise that the United States must act to promote reconciliation between Israel and at least some Arab leaders, and that the interests of no responsible party are served by further passage of time.

It is not obvious, though, that reconciliation is possible. The Middle East has been at war, sometimes hot and never less than cold, for nearly half a century. In 1948 war was midwife to the state of Israel with the expiration of the British mandate for Palestine (created in 1922 under the auspices of League of Nations). Arabs and Israelis fought again: on a large scale in 1956, when Israel joined forces with Great Britain and France to humble President Gamel Abdel Nasser of Egypt, in 1967, in 1973, and in 1982, and even more frequently on the more modest but still violent level of terror and response. This part of the world has not had much recent experience with peace.

But despite this history (and because of it too) there exists the strong belief that it is necessary and possible to solve the Arab-Israeli problem in a way acceptable to all the principal parties. Nevertheless, it must be asked whether this common view is correct. Is the Middle East dispute ripe for resolution? If so, why has a resolution not come about sooner, during the forty years since the state of Israel came into existence? What has changed? What form would the solution take, and how would the parties get there from here? What role should the United States assume? This first case study is addressed to these issues and related ones.

## From War to Uprising, 1967–1987

It took Israel just six days to defeat the armed forces of Egypt, Jordan, and Syria in June 1967. Israel came to control the territories along the West Bank of the Jordan River (formerly claimed by Jordan) and the Gaza Strip (administered by Egypt). Israel also gained (and later annexed) the Golan Heights, which had been Syria's, and brought under its sovereignty all of Jerusalem, combining what had been claimed by Jordan with what had been Israeli. In the process Israel took over not simply the land but its inhabitants: more than one million Palestinians. For the more than two decades since, Israel, the Arabs, the United States, and indeed the entire world have struggled with the political consequences of six days of military conflict.[2]

The last two decades are replete with examples of various schemes to bring about progress in the Middle East. One was the diplomacy of the first Nixon administration, notably the embrace of the Rogers Plan (named for Secretary of State William Rogers) for a comprehensive settlement of the entire Middle East question along the lines of United Nations Security Council Resolution 242. Another was the Carter administration's call with the Soviet Union in October 1977 for a conference in Geneva on the Middle East. The Camp David accords of 1978, the Reagan Plan of 1982, and the proposals put forth by Secretary of State George Shultz in 1988 were blueprints for an overall settlement of the region. Even American diplomacy in Lebanon, be it the efforts of the special negotiators or the presence of the marines, was held out as a necessary demonstration of the ability of the United States to broker diplomatic progress in the Middle East and prepare the way for a more comprehensive effort to follow.[3] Yet the history of American peacemaking efforts in the area is sufficiently mixed to justify asking why the territory-for-peace paradigm and American diplomatic activism retain their allure. With the important exception of the exchange brought about by the Camp David accords, no exchange of territory for peace has taken place.[4] Israel meanwhile has annexed Jerusalem and the Golan Heights and settled large parts of the West Bank.

To understand why more than two decades of peace efforts failed requires examining developments in both Israel and the Arab world. Within Israel one can point to a host of factors: the decline in the strength and appeal of the more conciliatory Labour alignment; the parallel rise of a nationalist Right and militant religious sentiment; the attachment of Prime Minister Menachem Begin to "Judea and Samaria" (the West Bank), which made it all but impossible for him to contemplate replicating on the West Bank what he had done with the Sinai at Camp David; the extreme national confidence that erupted in the wake of the 1967 war that blinded Israelis to the potential to translate their military gains into new and possibly lasting territorial and political arrangements; the brooding and self-doubt that emerged in Israel after the war of 1973 and especially after the Lebanese conflict (both reduced sharply any Israeli propensity to "take risks for peace"); the disillusionment with Egypt that took hold after Camp David, when Egypt and its president, Hosni Mubarak, appeared more interested in rejoining the Arab political fold than in adding substance to the new relationship with Israel; the long tenure (since 1984) of the divided and indecisive multiparty national unity government; and, most recently, the Palestinian *intifada* (uprising), which pushed talk of peace into the background while Israel grappled with this latest, qualitatively different challenge to its security.

The consequence of these developments is an Israel in which the return of the occupied territories is opposed by a large portion of the populace (the electorate is too volatile to characterize it with confidence as a majority). Israeli politics in the 1980s are a far cry from what they were just a decade earlier, when the Labour party could espouse to considerable public approval various plans to return much of the West Bank to Jordan. At issue today in Israel is not whether the Jordan River forms Israel's eastern defense boundary but whether it ought to form the country's eastern political boundary as well.

Israel's evolution, and the decline in its support for the territory-for-peace paradigm, is in part too a reaction to developments in the Arab world. Only Anwar Sadat was able to capitalize on the Arab "victory" in 1973 to negotiate with Israel. (The victory was less military than political and psychological, for the Arab armies were unable to exploit the initial advantages resulting from their unexpected attack, and were saved from a rout only by Soviet and American political intervention, which halted the fighting. All the same, the war restored a good deal of Arab pride.) Israelis were disappointed by the universal Arab rejection of Egypt and by Sadat's assassination, both of which bode badly for long-term ties between Egypt and Israel and for the prospects that other Arab leaders would risk as much for peace as did Sadat. That relations with Egypt never improved beyond a rudimentary level exacerbated matters. King Hussein, too weak to stay out of war in 1967, proved too weak to opt for peace after it. He often came to the brink only to pull back; although his caution was understandable and his ability to survive admirable, the former quality at least made Hussein a less than ideal partner in any peace process. A pact in February 1985 between Hussein and the PLO chairman, Yasir Arafat, "to move together" on the peace process came to nought when Hussein refused to act without the PLO's blessing, which proved impossible to get.[5] His neighbor to the north, Hafez el-Assad of Syria, proved an even worse partner for peace, for different reasons: Assad was unwilling to compromise on his demand for the complete return of the Golan Heights and, given Syria's claim to leadership in the Arab world, equally unwilling to compromise on the complete return of the West Bank and Gaza to Arab control.

Two other factors affecting Arab politics also explain why the territory-for-peace paradigm has fared poorly. The first relates to the Soviet Union. After 1967 the Soviets were intent on strengthening Syria's might and thereby their own influence in Damascus; similarly, the Soviet Union aided the PLO and wooed Hussein. Yet the Soviets refrained from restoring diplomatic relations with Israel, despite their ostensible interest in attending an international conference and Israel's insistence that the Soviet Union recognize it before the two nations could talk. Although there is some evidence that under Mikhail Gorbachev the Soviet Union is considering a shift in its policy (a Soviet delegation visited Israel in summer 1987 for the ostensible purpose of examining religious sites but in reality to initiate some political contacts, and senior Israelis, including Prime Minister Shamir, have met with high-level Soviet officials), Soviet policy toward the region since 1967 has emphasized criticism of American peacemaking efforts and armed support for several key Arab states. The principal result of this approach has been to maintain the perception in the Arab world that a military option exists and that time works for the radical Arab cause rather than against it.

Even more important as an explanation of why the Middle East dispute remains unresolved are the politics of the PLO. It has been a decade and a half since the PLO received an exclusive mandate to represent the Palestinian people from the Arab leaders who gathered in Rabat (Morocco) in autumn 1974. This collective Arab decision was noteworthy for nothing so much as for ensuring that Jordan would not be a viable negotiating partner for Israel. The principal Palestinian leader, Yasir Arafat, used the bulk of these years to gain international support for his cause, strengthen the PLO's military arm, and meet internal challenges to his authority. Until late 1988 he refused to renounce terror, accept Resolution 242 (on the grounds that it only treated the Palestinians as refugees and did not defend their desired right of self-determination), or recognize Israel and its right to exist, thereby failing to fulfill the traditional "requirements" of the United States for a dialogue and perhaps gain the opportunity to come to the bargaining table.[6] However understandable his decisions may have been in light of the movement's aims and internal dynamics, in reality they transformed the PLO into an organization that had the power to undermine the prospects for peace but not to contribute to them.

## December 1987 and Its Aftermath

The question arises, though, of whether the violence in the West Bank and Gaza that began in late 1987 and continued into 1989 has altered all political calculations. Quite possibly it has, for crises, even violent ones, have been known to stimulate diplomacy. But history is also replete with examples of conflicts that produced no negotiation and no spirit of compromise. The Middle East has seen both: 1973 being an example of the former, 1948 and 1967 examples of the latter.

Measuring the likely impact of the intifada requires first an analysis of the uprising itself. There were several likely causes. On one level, one can point to a successful guerrilla attack in November 1987 that killed six Israeli soldiers and seems to have emboldened the Palestinians, and to an accident in Gaza in early December 1987 (viewed as intentional by some locals) in which a truck driven by an Israeli killed a number of Palestinians. More fundamentally, the Palestinians were deeply frustrated with the occupation and afraid that it was becoming permanent, frustrated too with the apparent impotence of the PLO and the small degree of attention afforded the Middle East at recent Arab and Soviet-American summits, and increasingly resentful of their second-class political and economic status (this was particularly true among the young). In Gaza the growing appeal of fundamentalist Islam and the crowded conditions in the refugee camps may also have fueled the protests.[7]

The impact of the uprising is if anything even more complex than its causes. At a minimum it adds a new dimension to the Middle East conflict, which can be described as a Palestinianization of what had been previously a traditional interstate conflict. Israel now has to contend with the active hostility of many of the Palestinian Arabs living in Gaza and the West Bank (who number around one and a half million). In addition Israel must deal with the question of the allegiance of about 700,000 Israeli Arabs (Arabs living within the boundaries that circumscribed Israel before 1967 and their descendants, who are Israeli citizens although they do not serve in the armed forces), many of whom seem to be sympathetic to the Palestinians in the West Bank and Gaza.

The uprising's initial effect on Israel was to heighten its internal political polarization. The violence prompted some Israelis to conclude that the occupation is untenable, that it must be ended, and that some or all of the territories gained in 1967 should be returned to Jordan or incorporated into a Palestinian political entity. For other Israelis the uprising reinforced the appeal of politicians opposed to significant compromise. Any doubts that heightened polarization was the principal effect in Israel of the uprising was erased by the national elections of November 1988, which resulted in a divided vote and, after some six weeks of political maneuvering, again produced a "national unity" government in which the leading parties share power.

Just as important, the violence and the international response to it appeared to embolden the Palestinians, in the process prompting them and their leaders to conclude that time is on their side and that they are under no pressure to accept any proposal short of one that provides for an independent state. But they too are divided. Although the PLO leadership, after being caught unprepared for the outburst, regained a good deal of control, it does not enjoy unchallenged primacy. It must share power with Islamic fundamentalists (especially strong in Gaza), more radical Palestinian groups, and the local leadership, which has contributed to the uprising and been nurtured by it. Some Palestinians seem content with a state of their own, coexisting alongside Israel. Others, however, continue to reject Zionism and seek all of Palestine for their state.

No less important is the impact of the uprising on Jordan. King Hussein may have been the actor who lost the most from the violence, as his influence waned and his supporters found themselves intimidated and increasingly irrelevant. The uprising makes it all but impossible for Hussein to constitute his own Jordanian-Palestinian delegation that could negotiate with Israel; it may also have weakened his ability to construct a joint delegation with the PLO in which he would dominate rather than be a

figurehead. The result has been the disappearance, at least for the
time being, of the one diplomatic route that appealed to many of
Israelis (even if not a majority), namely the so-called Jordanian
option according to which Israel and Jordan would divide the
West Bank, allowing the Palestinians considerable political autonomy in the Jordanian portion.

It was in this context that Secretary of State George Shultz
decided to undertake a new diplomatic initiative. Shultz's mission of 1988 (or missions, for there were four trips in all between
February and June) were set in motion for several reasons. In part
Shultz's initiative was a political response, to help the Israelis
extricate themselves from a difficult situation. It was also an
opportunistic response intended to appeal to moderate Arab governments upset with the secret arming by the United States
of Iran. It was an emotional response to domestic and international pressures that the United States should not stand by in
the face of such violence. Finally, it was a calculated response
to the view that the uprising created new opportunities for diplomacy to prosper, given the Arabs' confidence and Israel's soul-
searching.

The substance of the initiative was revealed during the four
trips that Shultz made to the region in the first half of 1988.[8]
There were three principal elements: the United States would
endeavor with assistance from the secretary-general of the United
Nations to convene an international conference that would involve at a minimum the five permanent members of the Security
Council (including the Soviet Union), Israel, Jordan, and some
form of Palestinian representation in a joint delegation with Jordan; there would be immediate talks (intended to be completed
within six months) involving Israel and a Jordanian-Palestinian
delegation on interim, or "transitional," arrangements for governing the occupied areas, the arrangements to enter into effect three
months after the conclusion of the transitional talks and to last
for three years; and talks on the final status of the occupied
territories, scheduled to take no more than a year, would begin no
later than December 1988 (or some seven months after the in-

terim talks got under way), regardless of whether the parties had been able to agree on transitional political arrangements.

Other than as an expression of concern by the United States, the effort failed. Part of the fault lay in the formula itself. To shorten the transitional phase from the five years provided for in the Camp David accords to a maximum of three years—in effect accelerating the process—was to ignore that any such period is a time for the gradual building of mutual trust, which in time allows for more ambitious final arrangements to be made. To state that the talks on final status would begin regardless of the state of the interim negotiations not only shifted the focus of efforts to the most contentious issues but all but assured that any negotiations on interim arrangement would get nowhere once the linkage (and hence the leverage) was removed. To declare that the proposal was a whole that could not be changed in any part made the initiative appear as a diktat from the United States—which only increased Israel's propensity to resist. And to emphasize the international conference, in the best of circumstances a controversial idea, was especially controversial given that it was opposed by the prime minister of Israel and promoted by his foreign minister (and certain opponent) in the coming elections.

This last point leads one to examine the larger context, which perhaps offers a more basic explanation of why Shultz failed. The uprising not only emboldened Palestinians and unsettled Israelis but made both sides less inclined to negotiate. Questions of objectives aside, Palestinians were if anything less able than before to negotiate in the absence of clear and recognized local leadership (as it turned out, Palestinians on the West Bank refused to meet with Shultz), and the uprising also reduced Jordan's ability to act on behalf of the Palestinians. The initiative was weakened further by the status of the Israeli and American governments as lame ducks: both faced elections in November 1988.

There matters stood until July 31, 1988, when King Hussein again demonstrated his capacity to surprise, on this occasion announcing that Jordan would no longer bear responsibility for the West Bank. Declaring that "Jordan is not Palestine" (in the process rejecting the notion advanced by some Israelis that Jordan already constitutes the one Palestinian state needed in the region, in that a majority of its citizens are Palestinian), Hussein dissolved the lower chamber of Jordan's National Assembly (this chamber was oriented toward the West Bank) and ended most legal and administrative links between his country and the occupied areas. In effect Hussein declared the Jordanian option dead (along with peace initiatives ranging from the Reagan Plan of 1982 to Shultz's initiative of 1988), and handed responsibility for the people of the West Bank (and Gaza) to themselves and above all to the PLO.[9]

Not surprisingly, the immediate result of Hussein's announcement was to place enormous pressure on the PLO. The organization and its leadership could no longer hide behind the king; the Palestinian option had replaced the Jordanian option. Adding to the pressure was the continuing uprising—the PLO risked being supplanted by a new generation of actors if it could not demonstrate that it could accomplish something positive—and the counsel of the Soviet Union, Egypt, and Jordan. The time had come for the PLO to take the risk of showing some moderation, or risk instead being overwhelmed by others claiming they were better able to represent Palestinian interests.

The PLO reacted by sending out signs of flexibility. Typical was a statement made in mid-1988 by a senior official of the PLO close to Arafat suggesting the necessity for coexistence with Israel.[10] The United States reacted in turn, on the one hand expressing some interest in the expression of greater moderation, on the other pointing out what was still lacking in the PLO's formulations. (In 1975, as part of a package designed to induce Israel to pull back from lands taken from Egypt in 1967, the United States pledged that it would "not recognize or negotiate with the PLO so long as the PLO does not recognize Israel's right to exist and does not accept [United Nations] Security Council Resolutions 242 and 338." Renunciation of terror was a condition added later during the Carter administration.)[11] The uncertain authority of the PLO's statement only muddied matters more, as Arafat refused to endorse it unambiguously while other leaders of the PLO denounced it. To underline the point, the United States refused to recognize the declaration of statehood by the Palestinian National Congress on November 15, or let Arafat into the United States to address a session of the General Assembly on the Middle East, owing to his less than complete disassociation from terrorism.

The actions of the United States appeared to do some good when Arafat, in a meeting in Sweden on December 7 with a delegation of American Jews, stated that he "accepted the existence of Israel as a state in the region," rejected and condemned terrorism, and agreed to attend an international peace conference held on the basis of resolutions 242 and 338.[12] But a few days later in Geneva, where the special session on the Middle East of the United Nations General Assembly was being held after the United States refused to issue Arafat a visa, Arafat again seemed to backtrack. Not until a further statement the next day (December 14, 1988), at which time Arafat publicly and with little ambiguity met all three requirements imposed by the United States, did the United States agree to drop its self-imposed sanction against direct diplomatic contacts with the PLO and enter into a dialogue. The first meeting took place a few days later in Tunisia between leaders of the PLO and the American ambassador there.[13]

## Possible Solutions

The beginning of a dialogue between the United States and the PLO is a milestone, but it is not to be confused with a breakthrough.[14] Major, more difficult hurdles remain. Even so, the new dialogue imparts momentum to the search for a solution to the Middle East dispute. That said, the list of possible solutions to the Palestinian issue and to the larger issue of relations between Israel and the Arab states is long.

*The status quo.* The current situation is characterized by Israel's political and military control of the West Bank and Gaza Strip.

But this statement requires two qualifications: the control is less than complete, for few of the inhabitants accept it and there is regular violence. Second, no political arrangements are in place that are intended to be permanent: what exists is what has evolved since 1967. The status quo is popular with almost no one. Israelis are increasingly unhappy with the political, physical, and economic costs of occupation. What they cannot agree on is an alternative. Palestinians are if anything even more dissatisfied with current arrangements, although again there is disagreement on what should exist in their place. The main force supporting the status quo is simple inertia, for in the absence of consensus within Israel and the Palestinian community, as well as agreement between them, change will be hard to bring about.

*Annexation.* According to this option Israel would make formal and permanent what is now de facto and arguably temporary. What is in favor of this course is momentum; as noted in the influential Benvenisti Report of 1984, which examined developments in the occupied territories, "the political, military, socioeconomic and psychological processes now working toward the total annexation of the West Bank and Gaza Strip outweigh those that work against it."[15]

The problems that would greet any Israeli move to annex the territories would be great, however. The inhabitants would resist in every conceivable way; simply maintaining order would become a permanent nightmare. Israel would also find itself isolated internationally to a degree much greater than now. Annexation would also pose problems for Israel itself. Absorbing more than one and a half million Arabs with high birth rates—something that would make Jews a numerical minority within their own borders—would soon confront Israelis with a terrible choice. Either they would have to deny these people political rights, in which case Israel would cease to be a full democracy, or Jewish Israelis would be ruled by an Muslim and Arab majority. (Ironically, this last variant resembles nothing so much as a binational secular state, once promoted by some left-wing Jewish settlers during the British mandate and long the goal of many of the most radical, anti-Zionist Arab nationalists.)[16] Either way the social, cultural, and political principles of Zionism would be undermined by none other than the leaders of the Jewish state.

To avoid this outcome there is some talk of "transfer," mostly on the right fringe of Israeli politics. This is a euphemism for the annexation by Israel of the territories and the concomitant expulsion of the Palestinians across the Jordan River (that is, all the inhabitants but the small number of Jewish settlers). But this action too would have profound and almost certainly adverse consequences for Israel's well-being. If annexation of the land and people would jeopardize Israel's Jewishness, democracy, or both, "transfer" would jeopardize Israel's special claim to international support for reasons of history and morality. It would not satisfy the Palestinians, and it would almost certainly institutionalize the hostility between Israel and its neighbors.

*Two states.* This approach is one of partition. It would establish a second sovereign entity—a state of Palestine—in the area west of the Jordan River. In exchange for a right to exist in peace, Israel would hand back land that is now occupied, with precise boundaries to be negotiated according to demographic realities and Israel's security requirements. (The Palestinian state would however be likely to include Gaza and the most populated areas of the West Bank.) Also to be negotiated would be questions of what limitations would be placed on the military capabilities of the new state (if any), the status of Jerusalem (or at least arrangements governing access to the holy places), and the relations that the two states and Jordan would have after independence (possibly a three-way confederal arrangement akin to that enjoyed by Belgium, the Netherlands, and Luxembourg).[17]

The two-state solution would be one means of satisfying the intent of United Nations Security Council Resolution 242 and the territory-for-peace paradigm. It is in any event what most outsiders have in mind when they imagine a settlement to the Arab-Israeli dispute.[18] This outcome would satisfy some Palestinians but dissatisfy others, particularly those whose families had land in Israel before 1967, those with close ties to Syria or the other more radical states of the region, such as Libya, Iran, and Iraq, and those Palestinians in the embrace of fundamentalist Islam, who see Israel as little more than a twentieth-century version of the Crusaders, a Western outpost with no permanent right to exist in the Middle East. The approach might also lose support depending on the precise boundaries of the Palestinian state and the way the question of Jerusalem was dealt with.

The two-state solution would be welcomed by many Israelis eager to shed the costs of occupation and the demographic risk inherent in either annexation or the status quo, so long as the solution were accompanied by assurances about Israel's long-term security from the United States and possibly other parties (including Palestinian leaders).[19] Territorial adjustments and limits on the number and quality of arms to be allowed in the new Palestinian state would also alleviate concerns. But no amount of drafting or compromise is likely to assuage those Israelis who are settled in these lands or who see "Judea and Samaria" as being part of Israel's biblical legacy. Nor would this approach appeal to Israelis who fear that any Palestinian state west of the Jordan River—particularly one dominated by the PLO—constitutes a threat to Israel's well-being, either in itself or as the basis for a "second phase" of activity in which the objective would be to eliminate Israel altogether.

*Devolution.* This fourth option is an attempt to avoid the obvious shortcomings of the first two, as well as the difficulty of actually negotiating the third. Devolution too can be viewed as consistent with Resolution 242. It would confer on the inhabitants of the West Bank and Gaza a good degree of autonomy, or home rule. Devolution could be transitional—that is, a way station toward a separate state—or a permanent solution to the dispute. Either way devolution offers a political alternative that gives the Palestinians something less than a separate, sovereign state but something more than the status quo. It could be negotiated between Israel and Palestinian representatives or could come about from unilateral actions by each side.

Quite commonly the idea of devolution for the West Bank is linked to Jordan (although it need not be), an Arab state that already has a Palestinian majority. Parts of the West Bank would then become a special province, under Jordanian sovereignty, where considerable home rule (but not militarization) would be permitted. Parts of the West Bank would also become Israel's. All this would ease Israel's security concerns. At the same time, parallel change could take place in Gaza, although given the lack of historic links between Gaza and Jordan it is also possible that Gaza and its more than six hundred thousand inhabitants could gain some special international status (but not sovereign status).[20]

Devolution is likely to find considerable support in Israel. In part this is because the idea of devolution or autonomy itself is far from new. It has figured in the Israeli debate for more than twenty years, since the so-called Allon plan (named for Yigal Allon, then a leading figure in the Labour party and a deputy prime minister) provided for a small, autonomous, Palestinian province linked by a narrow corridor to Jordan, all but surrounded by territory that would be Israeli. Notions of autonomy are also central to the Camp David accords, which speak of an elected, "self-governing authority" and "full autonomy to the inhabitants" of the West Bank and Gaza, and to the Reagan Plan of 1982, which called for "self-government by the Palestinians of the West Bank and Gaza in association with Jordan."[21]

The staying power of the idea of devolution should come as little surprise. It is an attempt to provide an outlet for Palestinian political participation short of self-determination and a separate state, an outcome widely feared by the Israelis as an immediate threat to the security of their country and a long-term threat to its very being. Some Israelis hope that enough West Bank Palestinians will realize this option is the most they can expect to achieve and accept it, thereby lending it legitimacy, and that on seeing this Palestinian cooperation the world will conclude that the dispute has gone away.

The problem with this option is that there may be few Palestinians willing to embrace it. This was not always the case. It is quite possible that had Israel introduced meaningful autonomy into the occupied territories a decade ago it might have worked, in the process both isolating the more radical Palestinian groups and creating greater trust between moderate Palestinians and Israelis, which could have led in turn to greater degrees of self-rule and even a separate state. But Israel was unwilling to run the risk. Fearing anyone with nationalist pretensions, Israel frustrated (often by deportation) the emergence of a local Palestinian leadership that might have emerged as a legitimate interlocutor and alternative to the PLO. (Here Israel and the PLO ironically worked in parallel, for the PLO too lacked an interest in promoting an alternative to itself.) Some Israelis (especially on the Right) also opposed autonomy, believing it would inexorably lead to pressures for an independent state.

Much of this could change. Given the PLO's new international prominence and the heightened demands for a separate state, more Israelis may come around to favoring autonomy as a "less bad" option. Now, however, after two decades of activity by the PLO, the intifada, and the PLO's dialogue with the United States, it is possible that such a halfway measure may be seen as too little, too late by too many Palestinians and their supporters. King Hussein has made clear that he is not prepared to act on behalf of the Palestinians unless he is asked, something highly unlikely now or soon.[22] The result is that it is uncertain whether devolution remains viable as a permanent solution to the dispute between Israel and the Palestinians.

## The Middle East: A Case of Ripeness?

Any successful approach to the situation in the Middle East must blend Palestinian political requirements and Israeli security requirements. Expressed differently, two nationalisms must be accommodated. There is little evidence, however, that either nationalism is yet prepared to accommodate the other to a meaningful degree. As a result, the Middle East is not a dispute ripe for resolution. The first area where reality does not measure up to theory is that of outlook. Successful negotiation can come about only if leaders involved in a dispute conclude that compromise is preferable to the status quo. But here there is doubt on both sides. In the Arab world, and among Palestinians in particular, it is far from certain that there is a consensus to accept Israel as a permanent political entity—even if it is reduced to its borders of before 1967. For the more radical elements, continued struggle, even if it means forgoing any Palestinian political entity, state or otherwise, is preferable to compromising the ideal of a Palestinian state in all the land of Palestine. And for the more moderate, struggle may also prove preferable to accepting anything less than a state, or to accepting a state that includes less than the whole of the West Bank and Gaza, that is subject to severe constraints, or both.

There are similar questions about whether a majority in Israel favors substantial compromise. Although many Israelis are prepared to take risks for peace, many others prefer the current state of affairs, the military burdens notwithstanding, to the uncertainty of territorial compromise and the establishment of a new, Palestinian state. (More conservative Israelis even oppose schemes for significant autonomy or devolution, seeing them as constraining Israel's potential to annex areas of strategic importance while inevitably leading to pressures for a separate state.)[23] And even among those Israelis inclined to compromise, there is widespread opposition to giving back all the territories gained in 1967 and almost universal opposition to any change in the status of Jerusalem. For these people, the desirability of an alternative to the status quo would to a large extent be a function of the details.

Second, ripeness requires political leadership on both sides that is sufficiently strong to accept and sustain compromise. Again, the Middle East as currently configured falls short. In Israel there is no clear mandate for compromise and no consensus within the government as to what form compromise might take. The "national unity" government, unified in name and form only, is poorly equipped to undertake important initiatives or changes in policy. Not only is there a lack of direction, but there may be insufficient strength and resolve to face down domestic critics sure to resist any new policy that affects Israeli access to the occupied territories and control over them. The leadership situation is hardly better on the Arab side. Yasir Arafat is clearly the most popular leader in the Palestinian constellation and enjoys the backing of such states as Egypt, Saudi Arabia, and now Jordan. But he faces challenges from such states as Syria and Iran, from more radical factions in the Palestinian world, and from local leaders of the uprising itself.[24] In addition, the strong Islamic dimension of the uprising, particularly in Gaza, bodes ill for moderation.[25]

Third, there must be an acceptable formula. There is now precious little overlap between the positions being espoused by the Israelis and those of the Palestinians. Despite its divisions, Israel continues to be run by politicians who agree that there can be no separate Palestinian state, no negotiation with the PLO, no return to the boundaries that prevailed before 1967, and no change in Israeli sovereignty over all Jerusalem. All this is a far cry from even the views of the "pragmatists" of the PLO, who call for nothing less than a separate state that includes at least all the land occupied by Israel since 1967 (including "Arab" Jerusalem) and possibly all the additional territory that was to be part of the Arab state to be created alongside Israel in 1948 with the termination of the British mandate.[26] The question of Syria's claim to the Golan Heights (annexed by Israel) only increases the gap between what is being espoused by each side. Although a more forthcoming Arab approach toward the principal issues of the Middle East would almost certainly moderate Israel's often fickle public opinion, the maximum that Israel could be expected to propose in any peace package would appear to fall short of the minimum any Arab state or the PLO could be expected to accept.

Last, ripeness requires a commonly accepted approach to the negotiation. This also is missing. Israel's leaders are adamant that there be direct, face-to-face negotiations with their Arab interlocutors, but they are as yet unwilling to accept the PLO as the necessary interlocutor. One of Israel's principal political parties rejects an international conference, seeing little benefit in attending a gathering that includes a clear anti-Israeli majority. For its part the PLO prefers to take part in an international conference that would be attended by other Arab parties (presumably Jordan, Syria, and Egypt) as well as the members of the United Nations Security Council.

As if the above were not enough, making matters worse is the reality that the effort to bring peace to the Middle East is fragile. Any evidence that the PLO were associated with a terrorist incident would undermine its claim to have met the American conditions. Even a terrorist attack carried out by some faction of the PLO not sympathetic to Arafat and beholden to Syria, Iran, or Libya would harden Israeli attitudes and make it more difficult for any Israeli government to negotiate; indeed it is this possibility that makes such attacks so likely. Also disruptive would be an escalation of the violence in the occupied territories, be it because of actions taken by the Palestinians, by the Israelis, or both.

Just as important, the Palestinian issue does not exist in a vacuum. There are other scenarios involving Israel and any number of Arab states that could lead to a confrontation making compromise on this issue all but impossible for the leadership of any of the parties. A new round of fighting between Israel and Syria, an Israeli confrontation with Libya stemming from its accumulation of chemical weapons, a new Middle East conflict triggered by a specific issue, or simply the proliferation of advanced, destabilizing arms that induce preemptive strikes—one of these developments or some other could create an environment in which no dialogue over the Palestinian dispute could be sustained.

## A Policy for the United States

What, if anything, should the United States do in these circumstances? It can proceed along one of three paths. The government can wash its hands of the Middle East dispute, saying that it is hopeless, that there is no role for the United States, and that it is up to the local parties to reach an accommodation. It can also go to the other extreme, by placing its full weight and resources behind a diplomatic initiative designed to solve the dispute. Or it can work to ripen the situation, holding off ambitious diplomatic initiative until a number of changes come about. Each option deserves assessment.

The first option, that of holding back, or "benign neglect," has the advantage of apparent consistency with the bleak prospects for a solution. It may shock the local parties into doing more to make diplomacy possible. It also preserves the resources of the United States for other diplomatic challenges around the world that are more attractive candidates for attention. The problem with benign neglect is that it may turn out to be malign. The United States has too many interests in the Middle East, and the threats to them are too great, for it simply to focus its attention elsewhere. Drift can be dangerous in a part of the world known for terrorism where warring parties are accumulating not simply advanced conventional arms but also chemical and nuclear ones. In the absence of a diplomatic alternative, it is all too possible that those tending toward unilateralism and violence on all sides of the dispute would gain the upper hand.

As for the opposite approach, that of intense involvement on behalf of a comprehensive peace initiative, there are also arguments in its favor. Past initiatives by the United States have worked in the Middle East—witness the string of pacts brokered by the United States after 1973—and elsewhere. If left to themselves the parties will only drift into violence, but if steered they can perhaps move toward peace. Recent statements of the PLO and the opening of its dialogue with the United States suggest that there is a new readiness to make peace that must be explored and exploited. The problem with this approach is that it is simply too ambitious. As already shown, neither the PLO (despite its recent moves) nor the Israelis are ready to make the sort of compromises that the other would require. American efforts along these lines would only antagonize and possibly embolden those forces in Israel who say the United States cannot be trusted and that Israel must as a result take dramatic, decisive steps (such as annexing the territories) to ensure its long-term security in an untrustworthy and ultimately hostile world. Heightened American efforts would also produce more frustration than satisfaction among the Arabs over time, as it became evident that the United States could not deliver what they wanted. In the process the United States would be wasting precious diplomatic resources, not the least of which is its reputation as a sometimes effective arbiter of regional disputes. Most important, visible efforts by the United States for a comprehensive peace in the Middle East help perpetuate the illusion in the Arab world that the secret to peace in the region lies not in their own willingness to compromise but in an American willingness to pressure Israel.

How then can the United States avoid the pitfalls of doing too little or too much? Not by negotiating or promoting any specific settlement, but rather by creating a context in which a negotiation might succeed. What is called for is a policy of "ripening" designed, in the words of one thoughtful analyst, to "shaping the political environment" and "developing a commitment to negotiate."[27]

What would such a policy entail? To begin with, the United States should publicly and privately articulate what it considers the necessary principles guiding the Middle East peace process. The purpose is not to meddle in the internal politics of the disputants, but to work to change the thinking of the leaders and of the people they serve, thereby giving the leaders more latitude to compromise.[28] Key principles of an American strategy might resemble the following: the status quo is not only unstable but undermines the quality of life for Palestinians and Israelis alike; the territory-for-peace paradigm must guide efforts at peacemaking; there should not be any annexation of territory or transfer of the people now living in the occupied territories; there should be no new Israeli settlements in the territories; face-to-face talks (with or without third-party mediation) ought to form the heart of any diplomatic process; any arrangements concerning the final status of the region must be acceptable to the Palestinians and to Israel and Jordan; and some form of interim or transitional arrangements are necessary even in the absence of agreement about where they will lead and how long they will last.

These are intended as principles, not dictates. There is room for flexibility if need be. For example, if a dialogue indicated a degree of ripeness not otherwise evident, and if an international conference were a precondition of Arab participation in a political process, the United States could acquiesce even if the conference were little more than a vehicle to promote direct negotiations and if there were good reasons to believe that those taking part in it were prepared to make the effort a success.[29]

What should emerge is a set of dialogues—initially between the United States and Israel and the United States and the PLO, yet another involving the Israelis, the Palestinians living in the occupied territories, and perhaps other Palestinians—in which the United States worked to refine the thinking of the parties so that some overlap developed regarding the process of transferring authority for the occupied territories to the local inhabitants and their chosen leaders. It would be wise to hold off raising issues of what the final detailed shape of a Middle East settlement might be until after some self-rule had been introduced and the two parties had learned to work with each other. To the PLO the United States should say that nothing is ruled out (including a separate Palestinian state); to the Israelis that nothing is ruled in (including a separate Palestinian state). Preconditions to the contrary must be rejected—with the exception of Jerusalem, which will have to remain united if any Israeli government is to consider taking part in a dialogue.[30]

For some this will not be enough. As Harold Saunders has noted, "Many Palestinians would seriously consider a transitional authority if assured of greater freedom after a transitional period, but they would reject it as a cover for perpetual Israeli control."[31] There can be no guarantees, though; all the United States can say to the PLO and other Palestinians is that such arrangements are better than the status quo, and that they offer the only realistic path for convincing a majority of Israelis that an independent Palestinian state is not to be feared. This is a policy of realism, not idealism. Some would disagree with this last statement, believing that the United States has a strategic as well as a moral imperative to support Palestinian self-determination.[32] But the support of the United States for the principle of self-determination has never been unconditional; factors of history, viability, and national interest have always entered into the calculation. It remains to be see whether a viable Palestinian state could be created that did not pose a potential threat to both Jordan and Israel. But again, this is not yet an issue to confront. There is no Israeli government prepared to accept this outcome. And there is a strong case to be made for confronting only those issues for which a consensus might be fashioned while postponing those that are simply too difficult. For the foreseeable future the predicament of the Palestinians is one that cannot be solved, only managed.

The political environment could be improved (and the day brought nearer when such difficult issues could be raised) by introducing gestures intended to build confidence. The United States should insist that the PLO make good on its denunciation of terror. The PLO could also contribute to the prospects for peace by calling for a moratorium on all forms of violence within the occupied territories, by amending its charter of 1968, which describes both the partition of Palestine and the establishment of the state of Israel as "illegal,"[33] and by making clear that it regards a state as an end in itself and not as a springboard from which to gain all of Palestine.

The Israelis could also help to create an atmosphere in which the prospects for progress were removed. New settlements in the occupied territories could be eschewed, and the Israelis could pull back troops from some urban areas, eliminate or diminish the use of deadly force, and end the practices of deportation and long-term detention without trial. Allowing unconditional elections in the occupied territories so that the inhabitants could elect the representatives of their choice, whether for the purpose of self-rule, to choose diplomatic representatives, or both, would be an important gesture.[34] The Israelis could also go a long way toward making themselves a more viable negotiating partner by reforming their own electoral system, which now makes it all but impossible for any single party to fashion a mandate.

Any successful American policy would require continued support of Israel—political, economic, and military. Israel is likely to be receptive to American views, and open to taking risks, only if the government and the people believe that the United States is acting as a friend and will be with Israel in any crisis. An Israel that is unsure of the reliability or purposes of the United States will tend much more to unilateral acts and force as a substitute for diplomacy.

As noted earlier, the ability of the United States to ripen the setting for usefully considering the Palestinian issue could be undermined by larger hostilities in the region. The emergence of a new "intrastate" conflict has in no way eliminated the all too familiar conflict between Israel and the Arab states. Here too the United States must act. A key tenet of American policy toward the Middle East ought to be the nurturing of Israeli-Egyptian ties. More than any other development in the region for a generation, the return of the Sinai and the establishment of peaceful relations between Israel and Egypt have transformed the local political landscape. The prospects for full-scale war in the Middle East were immeasurably reduced by the drawing of an accepted border between Israel and what was (and could someday again be) the most militarily capable Arab state. American policy must therefore concern itself with promoting both the stability of President Mubarak's regime and a pro-Western attitude among the elite (including, if possible, tolerance for Israel). Substantial economic and military assistance must continue to flow from Washington to Cairo. Trade, investment, and educational and cultural ties should expand wherever possible.

It is also in the interest of the United States to continue a dialogue on the Middle East with the Soviet Union. The question is not whether to involve the Soviet Union in the Middle East—it is already involved, for better or worse—but how to shape its involvement. What is called for is not some formal Soviet-American diplomatic undertaking to solve the Middle East problem (such an initiative would likely fail, given differences in American and Soviet perspectives and, more important, the reality that neither great power has the capacity to "deliver" the local parties to the bargaining table) but rather a serious dialogue. In such a dialogue the United States could underline the dangers of continuing instability in the region and point out that the Soviet-American relationship will be affected by developments in the Middle East. There are things Moscow could usefully do that ought to be encouraged: it could make its political, economic, and military support for the PLO and Syria conditional on a moderating of their behavior, restore diplomatic relations with Israel, and endorse principles akin to those suggested above for the United States.

All this would represent a considerable change. For years it was assumed that the Soviets had little interest in promoting stability in the region, because only their dispute with Israel and a need for arms gave Arab states and the PLO reason to be close to the Soviet Union. Now, however, there is evidence that Mikhail Gorbachev and those around him see reason to promote diplomatic progress in various regional disputes, perhaps to buy breathing space at home on the basis of accomplishment abroad or to avoid a costly and dangerous regional competition with the United States. This willingness should be tested. Even if the Soviets' "new thinking" turns out not to be so new, there is always something to be gained if Washington and Moscow have a better understanding of each other's interests and intentions. Such knowledge can help avoid crises or, if they occur, facilitate their management.

There is good reason too to ensure that any such dialogue between the two powers encompass the potential proliferation in the region of chemical and nuclear arms and advanced delivery systems. There exists not only a common interest in slowing these developments but some opportunity to slow them. (There may be more promise in working directly with the states of the region, either by persuading them to eschew certain systems or by having them agree to a regime of confidence-building measures, such as providing advance notice of any missile flight tests. Here too, though, there is a potential role for the Soviet Union to play.)[35] The use of chemical weapons in the Iran-Iraq War, Saudi Arabia's purchase from China of surface-to-surface missiles, Israel's development of nuclear weapons—these and other new dangers warrant greater attention from both the United States and the Soviet Union.

None of this promises to solve the Palestinian problem or the larger set of disputes that divide Israel from the Arabs. These disputes are simply not ready to be solved, or at least those who lead the key parties are neither ready nor able to solve them. To ignore this reality and to seek a comprehensive and lasting resolution of the dispute threatens to be not simply futile but counterproductive, for the attempt and its certain failure would stimulate and embolden those who have no long-term stake in compromise. The goal of the United States must be to nurture an environment in which moderates emerge and negotiations can prosper. By preaching realism and restraint, by supporting its friends so they will feel secure and others will know that there is no alternative to compromise, by encouraging steps to promote confidence, and by providing a mechanism for discussions that could one day lead to fruitful negotiations, the United States can do this.

# 3

## GREECE, TURKEY,

## AND CYPRUS

There are strong parallels between the relationship of Israel to its Arab neighbors and that of Greece and Turkey, although the latter pair are both formal allies of the United States and members of NATO. Again the United States finds itself attempting to nurture close relations with two parties that are in close proximity but at odds with each other. Greek-Turkish disputes not only threaten important American and Western interests in the eastern Mediterranean, but complicate the larger task of managing the Atlantic alliance.

There is little in this that is fundamentally new. When they met after World War II, the founders of the Atlantic alliance were reluctant to include Greece and Turkey in their new military organization. It was argued that to embrace them would be to embrace their rivalries, in the process blurring the Atlantic and Continental focus of the new alliance by taking in states more a part of the Balkans, the Mediterranean, and the Middle East. Some feared that the new organization possessed too few resources to absorb additional responsibilities. Many worried that Greece and Turkey lacked the requisite cultural, social, and historical ties to the West to become useful members of NATO. But within three years of NATO's creation in 1949 these doubts were overcome, less by choice than by strategic necessity.

More than thirty years after Greece and Turkey joined NATO, American interests in both countries remain substantial. Strategic considerations are still paramount. Turkey's army, NATO's second largest, is in a position to tie down a significant element of the Warsaw Pact's ground forces; Turkey's control of the Bosporus and Dardanelles will be critical if in a crisis NATO is to prevent the Soviet Union's Black Sea Fleet from gaining access to the Mediterranean, where Soviet ships could challenge the U.S. Navy's Sixth Fleet. Greek air and naval facilities contribute to American control of the Mediterranean. Together Greece and Turkey provide a basis for the United States to project military force on and around the European continent during both peacetime and war. In addition, Turkey is central to the planning of the United States in the theater comprising the Persian Gulf and Southwest Asia; its large ground forces and numerous airfields (providing a potential site for tactical air operations by the United States) complicate Soviet planning for any use of force in the area.[1]

The importance of Greece and Turkey and developments in the eastern Mediterranean transcend local military, political, and economic concerns. The United States has a major stake in maintaining the cohesion of the Atlantic alliance. Tensions in the southern flank only add to the centrifugal forces that weaken deterrence. Two important sources and consequences of these tensions are the unstable situations in Cyprus and the Aegean, which could provoke armed confrontation between Greece and Turkey. It is possible to envision scenarios, possibly starting with some incident along the "green line" separating the divided island's Greeks and Turks, in which Greek Cypriots conclude with the mainland Greeks that they have no option but to arm themselves further and accept additional forces from Greece. Such a step could lead the Turkish government to reinforce its own positions on Cyprus, and the stage would be set for another crisis on this island. An Aegean confrontation is even easier to envision given all the contested boundaries and the frequency of military exercises conducted in the region by both Greece and Turkey. The Aegean is an accident waiting to happen.

Amid such tensions there are sure to be renewed pressures for the United States to become more involved in the region, either to solve disputes in Cyprus or the Aegean or to satisfy the many demands of Athens and Ankara. It is not at all certain, however, that the prerequisites are in place for American diplomatic activism. The United States should instead follow a more modest policy of conflict management, to prevent the breakdown of regional order and promote developments that might create conditions in which more traditional and ambitious diplomacy could eventually succeed.

## The Aegean

The Aegean Sea is a source of tension between Greece and Turkey and a factor complicating American relationships with both countries. There the Greeks believe their interests to be most threatened by Turkey, whereas for Turkey the Aegean is the "other" area (beside Cyprus) where it believes it is discriminated against. As a consequence, the Aegean and the morass of technical yet highly charged issues it encompasses constitute the second major cause of friction between Greece and Turkey. The term "Aegean" is a shorthand for a set of issues contested by the two countries.[2] Many claims go back more than sixty years, to treaties that Greece interprets as giving it the right to station military forces on Greek islands adjacent to Turkey (most notably the island of Limnos), but that Turkey interprets otherwise. Greece points out the incongruity of NATO's not being able in peacetime to defend territory that it must protect in wartime; Turkey stands by its reading of relevant treaties and refuses to budge, fearful that any compromise would weaken its stance vis-à-vis the entire range of contested Aegean issues. This matter is at the heart of Greece's refusal to participate in NATO exercises, for it insists first on receiving a de facto endorsement from NATO of its position.

A second Aegean issue involving NATO directly concerns the division of command and control responsibilities for the region.

Greece, which left NATO's military wing between 1974 and 1980 in anger at NATO's failure to discipline Turkey for its intervention in Cyprus, wants a return to the command arrangements existing before 1974, which gave it total oversight of the Aegean. Turkey's desire to share the oversight is refused by Greece, which opposes the precedent of Turkey controlling anything Greek. The standoff reduces NATO's efficiency in the region and brings about the far from ideal situation of having command of the area directed from a NATO headquarters in Italy.[3]

Three of the differences in the Aegean surround legal claims. There is no agreement on what constitutes the Aegean continental shelf. Turkey is asking for joint exploration of the shelf; Greece, defining the shelf differently along lines dictated by Greek islands, wants exclusive control of the shelf and any resources it might contain. Greece, while claiming a territorial sea of six nautical miles around its many islands, reserves the right to extend this claim to twelve miles. Turkey has stated publicly that it would view any such change in the Greek position as a casus belli, for it would effectively close most of the sea to Turkish warships. Thus far Greece has held off asserting this broader claim in practice. There are similar disputes over airspace; in this instance Turkey refuses to recognize Greece's ten-mile limit, and to be sure the Greek government does not miss the point, Turkish fighters regularly challenge the Greeks on this matter.

It is difficult to imagine "solving" the tangle of issues that make up Greek-Turkish differences over the Aegean. What accounts for this lack of ripeness, however, is not the absence of a formula: for example, Turkey could accept partial militarization of Limnos in exchange for more modest Greek claims to territorial sea and airspace, some formula could be devised for sharing the continental shelf, and Turkey could agree to have the World Court decide the issue of the shelf in exchange for Greece dropping its opposition to Turkey's desire to join the European Economic Community (EEC). But this misses the point. It is not so much Aegean issues that create tension between Greece and

Turkey as tensions between Greece and Turkey that make it all but impossible to resolve specific differences. Each government believes its interpretation of laws and treaties to be absolutely correct, and each would encounter massive domestic political resistance if it were seen to be compromising anything of importance on issues so close to the core of national identity and security.

The time is far from ripe for a breakthrough. Any initiative would end in frustration while earning the enmity of both sides, neither of which feels any urgency to alter long-standing positions. Making things still more complicated is the reality that neither Greece's leadership nor Turkey's may be sufficiently strong to withstand the public outcry that would be sure to greet any compromise. Although it is possible that a dramatic foreign policy accomplishment could shore up governments increasingly under siege for their handling of domestic matters, it is more likely that neither leadership will conclude it has a mandate to undertake such steps in the first place, or the political support to survive them.

For diplomacy to prosper would probably require a number of developments. Governments would have to enjoy more popularity at home, which would in turn require improved economic situations. At the same time (or conceivably as an alternative) the costs of not compromising would have to increase markedly, so that even weak governments would be unable to resist negotiation. This could result from an increased danger of armed conflict —which might cause leaders to recalculate the cost of their current positions—or from a reordering of priorities, for example a Turkish decision to forgo its Aegean interests in exchange for Greece's dropping of its opposition to Turkey's joining the EEC. For the foreseeable future, however, no changes of such magnitude appear likely, and the prospects for diplomacy are poor.

But this does not mean that nothing is to be done; the stakes and the likelihood of a confrontation between the two countries are too high. A crisis was only just avoided in spring 1987, after the Greek government decided to nationalize the North Aegean

Petroleum Company. This decision was viewed in Ankara as possibly presaging a renewed Greek exploitation of the disputed continental shelf, in contravention of the Bern Agreement of 1976, and Turkey sent but then halted a research vessel dispatched to explore for oil in the part of the shelf claimed by Greece. Both governments moved to the brink of confrontation; an outbreak of fighting was prevented only by external appeals for restraint from the United States and several West European governments, and uncertainty on the part of both Greece and Turkey about what would happen if shooting began.

One positive result of the crisis was to contribute to the decision by Prime Minister Papandreou of Greece and Prime Minister Ozal of Turkey to meet in Davos, Switzerland, in early 1988. Other factors may also have helped to bring about a summit: a mutual interest in increased trade and tourism, the Turkish desire for membership in the EEC, which Greece could prevent, a Greek desire to undo Turkish occupation of a substantial part of Cyprus. But more than anything it was this brush with confrontation and a desire to avoid future conflicts that brought together the two leaders.

The face-to-face session was something of an accomplishment in itself. In addition, the two leaders agreed to set up two working groups—one on economic cooperation, the other on outstanding political issues—and to hold future summits regularly. (The next one was held at the Greek resort of Vougliagmeni in June 1988, making Turgut Ozal the first Turkish prime minister to visit Greece in some thirty-six years.) And the meeting also produced one substantive benefit on the political and military side: a decision to establish a Greek-Turkish "hot line," modeled on the Soviet-American one. Should another incident occur in the Aegean—were some plane to enter the airspace of the other country or some aircraft or ship to shoot at a plane or ship of the other—a dedicated communications link between responsible authorities of each country could well prevent military escalation.

But the significance of the near crisis of spring 1987 and the diplomacy at Davos in its aftermath ought not to be exaggerated.

The two did not produce any discernible change in the basic policy positions or either Greece or Turkey, nor bring about a far greater desire for agreement. Instead the experiences seem to have increased the disposition on all sides to improve consultations and better manage the relationship. This is an accomplishment, both as a commitment to avoid crises and as an exercise that with time could engender greater trust, but of itself it does not signify that either Athens or Ankara is now ready to compromise basic stances. A direct attempt to solve the Aegean dispute is unlikely to succeed. The problem is not an absence of possible compromises that would protect the essential national interests of both countries. Nor is it a lack of negotiating approaches: the International Court of Justice is available for some aspects of the problem, direct talks with or without third parties are available for others. Instead the principal obstacle to an Aegean pact appears to be the nature of the two governments most involved. Neither is confident of its own future; both are vulnerable to popular passions and a lack of realism that would make any possible agreement controversial at best and unsustainable at worst. To manage the status quo so that war does not result may be the preferable course of action.

It is not difficult to add to the agenda for future meetings between Greece and Turkey. Beyond expanding such activities as trade, investment, and tourism and breaking down cultural and political stereotypes (reinforced, for example, by biased textbooks), one natural possibility would be for Greece and Turkey to adapt for their use in the Aegean the Soviet-American Agreement on the Prevention of Incidents on and over the High Seas (1972).[4] This agreement, which has served the superpowers quite well, stipulates rules of the road for their navies when they are near each other on the high seas. The intent is to avoid acts of harassment or challenge that could result in an incident, and the principles could easily be applied in the Aegean.

Second, given the large number of contested areas in the Aegean, Greece and Turkey would benefit from a procedure by which each would in advance notify the other of the timing, location, and size of air and naval exercises. Here the relevant model is final act of the Conference on Security and Cooperation in Europe (CSCE, or Helsinki Agreement), which stipulates for advance notification of exercises and the exchange of observers (many of these are voluntary, but they could just as easily be made mandatory in the Aegean). The bilateral agreement reached after Davos not to conduct maneuvers in the Aegean during peak tourist months is a step in the right direction. So too would be the adoption by Greece and Turkey of a version of the Agreement on the Prevention of Dangerous Military Activities reached by the United States and the Soviet Union in June 1989, which sets forth procedures for minimizing the chances that accidental military contacts will grow into large-scale confrontations.

What these suggestions have in common is modesty. They are not intended to resolve the Aegean problem, which for the foreseeable future will resist resolution, but rather to help manage a situation fraught with potential danger for Greece and Turkey, and for all those with a stake in peaceful relations between them. In the process, they not only would contribute to the stability of the region but could help create conditions in which more ambitious diplomacy might succeed.

## Cyprus

The island of Cyprus and its seven hundred thousand inhabitants are central to the politics of the eastern Mediterranean. Along with the Aegean, Cyprus accounts for most of the tensions between Greece and Turkey and complicates American relations with each. Aid programs, negotiations over bases, and the coherence of NATO all suffer because of the Cyprus problem. To make matters worse for the West, the Soviets are increasing their efforts to exploit this Western standoff for their own purposes. Moreover, its proximity to both Europe and the Middle East makes Cyprus itself of strategic importance. Not surprisingly, the question arises of where Cyprus is heading and what the response of the United States should be.

As is often the case, history offers a guide. Few of the thirty years of the Republic of Cyprus have been free of intercommunal strife in one form or another. Just a few years after it gained independence in 1960, the young republic found itself on the brink of civil war. Amid rising clashes between the Greek and Turkish communities on the island (in which the Turkish minority usually fared poorly), the Turkish military went on alert to deter the Greek Cypriots and their supporters in Athens from escalating their attacks on Turkish Cypriots. To forestall any such Turkish military intervention, President Lyndon Johnson dispatched a harsh, threatening letter to Prime Minister Ismet Inonu of Turkey. In the strongest possible terms, described by Undersecretary of State George Ball as "the most brutal diplomatic note I have ever seen" and as "the diplomatic equivalent of an atomic bomb," the letter set out to dissuade the Turks from intervening. The letter went so far as to say, "I hope you will understand that your NATO allies have not had a chance to consider whether they have an obligation to protect Turkey against the Soviet Union if Turkey takes a step which results in Soviet intervention, without the full consent and understanding of its NATO allies."[5] The undiplomatic missive had the desired effect—Turkey did not use military force in the crisis of 1963–64—although at the cost of introducing permanent resentment into the Turkish-American bilateral relationship.

A decade later Cyprus once more moved to the brink, and this time the majority of the island's people were not so fortunate. A coup in the Cypriot capital of Nicosia in July 1974, inspired in large part by the military junta in command in Athens, overthrew Archbishop (and President) Makarios and briefly brought to power a right-wing Cypriot regime distinguished by its involvement in anti-Turkish terrorism and a desire for *enosis* (unification of all Cyprus with Greece). This time there was no letter from the United States, unsympathetic to Makarios and distracted almost

entirely by the final agonies of Watergate. Whether any such letter might have deterred Turkey a second time is doubtful; Henry
Kissinger, then the secretary of state, later suggested that the
United States could have done nothing short of threatening military action that would have dissuaded Turkey from intervening.
In his words, "Turkey was not interested in a negotiated solution;
it was determined to settle old scores."[6]

In any event Turkey intervened soon after the coup in July that
ousted Makarios, gained a foothold on the island, agreed to a
cease-fire, and then decided that further military action was preferable to leaving the fate of the Turkish Cypriots in the hands of
either the diplomats meeting in Geneva or those Greek Cypriots
who might return to rule in Nicosia. In August Turkey exploited
its local military superiority and took approximately 40 percent
of the island for the Turkish Cypriot minority. Through massive
population shifts, the Turkish military brought about the effective partition of Cyprus into a Turkish Cypriot North and a Greek
Cypriot South.[7]

Since the violent summer of 1974 the island has remained
divided, with the Turkish Cypriot minority (about 20 percent of
the total population) occupying nearly 40 percent of the island,
including some of its most desirable territory. Turkish military
action replaced the patchwork of Greek and Turkish settlements
that divided the island into separate Greek and Turkish zones
while producing a large number of refugees. Despite a strong
record of economic growth few Greek Cypriots, whether displaced
or not, are satisfied with the resulting status quo. Control by the
Turkish Cypriots of a disproportionate piece of a divided Cyprus
is viewed as unjust; the presence of 25,000 mainland Turkish
soldiers in the North (or more, according to some estimates) only
exacerbates frustrations. So too did the declaration of independence in November 1983 by the Turkish Cypriots, a development
thus far recognized by Ankara alone. Little of this frustration
with the current situation is shared by the Turkish Cypriots, who
under the leadership of Rauf Denktash are enjoying the fruits of
1974: de facto independence and self-determination, if not pros-

perity. Together with their patrons in Ankara they are masters of their own territory, regardless of how small, isolated, or poor it might be. In the eyes of the Turkish Cypriots the mainland Turkish soldiers are an insurance policy, welcomed initially as liberators and now as protectors.

This difference in perspective is duplicated in the respective views of history of the two communities. The Turkish Cypriots draw their lessons from the early years of Cypriot independence, when the Turkish minority suffered physically, politically, and economically at the hands of the Greek Cypriot majority. The events of 1974 confirmed the Turkish minority's belief that they could not place their trust in their fellow islanders or leave their own welfare to them. The Greek Cypriots too were dissatisfied with the Cyprus of 1960–74, but only because the Turkish minority was able to frustrate their ability to govern. This frustration is in large part what led Makarios in 1963 to propose amending the constitution in ways that would have weakened the veto power of the minority. Just as predictably, the Greek Cypriots today focus on the injustice inherent in the island since 1974.[8]

In this debate between Greek and Turkish Cypriots the two motherlands are deeply involved. In addition to former mainland Turks and Turkish soldiers in the North are several thousand Greek soldiers in the South. (Both the Republic of Cyprus, that is, the Greek Cypriots, and the "Turkish Republic of Northern Cyprus" also have their own small military forces. The Greek Cypriot force, however, is larger and more capable.) The flow of trade and investment from Greece and Turkey to their respective zones in Cyprus is considerable; the flow from Turkey is especially heavy because subsidies are essential of the economically weak and isolated North is to survive as a distinct entity. Politically, Greece and Turkey each possess significant influence (but not control) over developments in Cyprus. Neither Greece nor Turkey can afford to appear less than stalwart in its support of its Cypriot community; the same applies to prominent politicians in both countries. One consequence of these ties between mainlands and island is that Cyprus occupies a central place in what there is of the Greek-Turkish relationship. It casts a pall over all else. For Greece Cyprus symbolizes the potential threat posed to other Greek interests by Turkey; for Turkey it symbolizes the basic hostility of the Western world to Turkish interests.

With so much at stake it is understandable that many have sought to bridge the differences that divide the island. All such efforts have run aground on the basic issues of how political power and territory are to be distributed between the two Cypriot communities. For the Turkish side the principles that cannot be compromised are equality, federalism, and bizonality. These three demands can be interpreted as a desire for widespread powers, including veto power for the Turkish Cypriots in any national government, considerable autonomy, and continued geographic expression of their autonomy in the form of a Turkish Cypriot province or state within a federal republic of Cyprus. For the Greek Cypriots the guiding principles are territorial recovery, the rights of individuals to return to their former homes, and the need to restore the political primacy of the majority within a federal system in which executive power remains considerable.

To this already complicated set of demands must be added several others. Greek Cypriots insist that Turks who settled in Cyprus after 1974 return to the mainland, which no Turkish or Turkish Cypriot leadership could endorse. Perhaps more important, the Greek Cypriots, backed staunchly by the government in Athens, want all mainland Turkish troops out of Cyprus as soon as possible. Greek Cypriots and their supporters everywhere view the Turkish military presence as a chief cause of current problems. The Turkish Cypriots see the presence of Turkish troops as a consequence of deep-seated political problems inherent in the makeup of Cyprus. They thus resist the notion of even partial withdrawal until satisfactory political safeguards have been established and implemented.

At the same time, the Turkish side opposes any political approach to solving Cyprus's dilemma that does not explicitly confirm Turkey's continuing role as a guarantor. (Turkey, along with Greece and Great Britain—as the former colonial power

—were designated the three guarantors of the provisions and treaties that established an independent Cyprus in 1960. Turkey cited its status as a guarantor as the legal basis for its later intervention.) For Turkish Cypriots and mainland Turks alike, a key lesson of the period 1960–74 on Cyprus is that Turkey must retain a special role if Turkish Cypriots are to prosper; Greek Cypriots resist such a notion, arguing that granting Turkey the status of a guarantor will only ensure a second Turkish military intervention.

Despite these and other, less significant differences, it is possible to sketch the outlines of a comprehensive solution to the Cyprus dispute. Such a package might consist of the following basic elements: a single federal government with one international personality, dominated by Greek Cypriots but with Turkish Cypriots holding important offices and delineated veto powers; two state governments, each possessing considerable autonomy; essential bizonality, with controls on the rights of refugees to return to their former homes; a Turkish sector reduced from its current size to one taking up 25 to 30 percent of the island, with the once flourishing city of Varosha and its environs returned to the Greek Cypriot province; a phased withdrawal of Turkish and Greek forces, their number to be reduced to a level acceptable to both sides according to a mutually acceptable timetable; continued guarantor rights for at least Turkey and Greece; and provisions for peacekeeping forces and the like, to monitor the specifics of the arrangement.

Doubtless both Greek and Turkish Cypriots could find fault with elements of this proposed solution. Nevertheless, it could meet the minimum requirements of the two communities, recognizing that many of the most difficult points of contention could be decided only at a level of considerable detail. It would also avoid other options that virtually everyone with a stake in the dispute agrees are unacceptable. Neither Greece nor Turkey would accept the "other" mainland absorbing the entire island, and this prospect would be equally unacceptable to Greek Cypriots and Turkish Cypriots. Also unacceptable to most Cypriots (who possess a normal degree of nationalism) is a so-called double enosis, according to which Greece would absorb the south of Cyprus and Turkey the north. Making the current division permanent—in effect recognizing the "Turkish Republic of Northern Cyprus"—would alienate permanently all Greeks and Greek Cypriots, with assuredly adverse consequences.

If all the options are unattractive, the future for Cyprus is either the status quo or some form of reunification. Progress in the direction of the latter, though, would require Greece, Turkey, and the two Cypriot communities to compromise. Unfortunately the parties have thus far been unwilling to do this. This intransigence drove one veteran diplomat to characterize Cyprus as follows: "I know of no problem more frustrating or more bedeviled by mean-spiritedness and lack of mutual confidence, nor of a problem where all concerned would so obviously gain from a reasonable settlement."[9]

The reasons for the impasse are not limited to one side or the other. The absence of ripeness stems from a number of factors, and clearly goes beyond anything having to do with formulas. The Turkish Cypriots are relatively comfortable with the present set of arrangements, despite economic hardship and political isolation. Since 1974 they have known not only unprecedented physical security but also political satisfaction. They place little faith in promises of political equality and even less in physical guarantees not emanating from Ankara. They are also confident that the world will grow weary of the Cyprus problem and come to recognize that the state of affairs prevailing since 1974 not only is preferable to that which preceded it, but also is here to stay.

This perception is largely shared by Ankara. Many Turks argue that given the relative stability that has come to Cyprus since 1974, a return to the status quo ante makes little sense. And the Turks are proud of what Denktash and the Turkish Cypriots have accomplished. The military, remembering the difficulties it encountered in its landings in 1974, has little appetite for withdrawing troops and raising the prospect of another forced entry. Last, many Turks view the division of Cyprus as inevitable owing to the inability of Greeks and Turks to live comfortably together.

They have difficulty understanding what all the fuss is about, and why anyone would suggest that reunification would be more stable and peaceful than separate development.

Turkey does have at least one important incentive to promote diplomatic progress on Cyprus that the Turkish Cypriots do not have. Because of the influence of the U.S. Congress, Cyprus is a millstone around the neck of Turkey, one that jeopardizes Turkey's relationship with its most important ally. Every year Congress reduces the administration's request for economic and military aid to Turkey. Even so, Ankara is not anxious to press the pace of diplomacy or troop withdrawal. The Turks have little confidence that Congress would change its attitude toward Turkey even if the Cyprus problem were solved. Some Turks look at the combined potential strength of left-wing parties in the north and south of Cyprus and see no reason to press for a reunification that would only raise the prospect of a hostile government controlled by Greek Cypriot leftists and supported by their Turkish Cypriot counterparts.

Moreover, even if the government of Turkey were inclined to compromise, it is not certain it could convince the Turkish Cypriot leader, Rauf Denktash. Despite all the leverage Turkey derives from its military presence and economic subsidies and despite what Greeks and Greek Cypriots believe, Denktash and those around him enjoy autonomy and room for maneuver. The revival of Turkish democracy and the strength of Turkey's press ensure that Denktash's voice will be heard, and woe to any mainland politician who can be portrayed as compromising the interests of Turkey and Turkish Cypriots simply to placate the United States.

The Greek Cypriots should have the greatest incentive to promote diplomatic progress to reunify their island. For years, however, President Spyros Kyprianou of Cyprus sought to steer a difficult but above all cautious middle path, partly to avoid offending staunch Hellenists and, in particular, the still powerful Orthodox church, which opposes giving away territory and political power simply to see the country reunified in name only. These groups would prefer undiluted authority in the 60 percent of the land they now hold to substantially reduced authority in a nominal republic covering the entire island and all its inhabitants. Organizations representing various refugee groups oppose any formulation of an overall agreement that does not permit refugees to return to their homes. At the same time, Kyprianou was under pressure from an informal coalition of Cypriot Communists (who constitute the largest single party in the South) and center-right politicians that favored a more accommodating approach toward the Turkish Cypriots. The mainland Greek government further complicated the task of any Cypriot president with its strident anti-Turkish rhetoric, public criticism of proposals by the United Nations, and insistence that all Turkish soldiers be removed from Cyprus as a first step in any political process. It remains to be seen whether Kyprianou's successor, George Vassiliou, can carve out for himself greater running room, notwithstanding his impressive victory in the presidential election of February 1988.

It is thus easy to comprehend why the dogged diplomatic efforts of the United Nations secretary-general, Javier Pérez de Cuellar, have failed to yield a political settlement. One initiative, begun in 1984, was built around a framework intended to be acceptable to both communities. A summit in January 1985 between Kyprianou and Denktash soured when the former rejected a good deal of what had been negotiated beforehand; a version of the framework put forward in spring 1986 was also rejected by the Greek Cypriots, allegedly because it went too far in protecting minority interests. In between, in April 1985, Denktash was cool to revisions of the original framework that he saw as compromising the essential interests of his community. Even should this impasse be broken, using the "outline proposals" put forth in January 1989 by President Vassiliou of Cyprus, it is difficult to see how the United Nations could lead the parties much further in light of all that divides them on the issues and all the political factors that work to frustrate statesmanship and compromise.

One can imagine procedural alternatives to the approach recommended by the United Nations. President Kyprianou of Cyprus, who increasingly came to regard the efforts of the United Nations as hostile to his interests and as favoring the Turkish Cypriots, voiced support for two possibilities: either another high-level meeting between him and Denktash, or, if this was not possible, an international conference that would be called to consider all aspects of the Cyprus problem. Yet it is difficult to discern much that is attractive about either prospect. A high-level meeting convened without much preparation and agreement—in short, without the consensus sought unsuccessfully for the last several years by the United Nations—would likely accomplish little. Notwithstanding friendly atmospherics, the summit of August 1988 in Geneva between President Vassiliou of Cyprus and Denktash made little progress beyond setting an ambitious deadline of June 1, 1989, for a settlement and agreeing to a new round of talks in Nicosia.[10]

An international conference would only complicate matters further by adding new participants and publicity. It is interesting that this last proposal dovetails with the Soviet proposal for Cyprus of January 1986, which calls for a unitary Cyprus with a structure to be determined through negotiations. Two parts of the proposal are patently self-serving: the call for the island's demilitarization, which would eliminate the British sovereign base areas, and that for an international conference in which the Soviet Union, as a permanent member of the United Nations Security Council, would be represented.[11] It is thus not at all obvious that inviting the Soviets into a dispute involving major Western interests and several NATO allies would serve anyone's interests but Moscow's and its communist associates in Cyprus.


## A Policy for the United States

With important interests at stake, the United Nations running out of ideas, and unpromising alternatives beginning to surface, some suggest that the United States should mount a major diplomatic effort to solve the Cyprus problem; Greek-

Americans and their supporters in Congress have been particularly outspoken on this point. Camp David is often cited as an example of what concerted American diplomacy can accomplish even in the most difficult and complex situations.

But both the idea and the analogy are flawed. Those who point out that there are few substitutes for American diplomatic leadership must recognize that there is no substitute for having the disputants themselves willing parties to bargain in good faith and make difficult, courageous decisions. This is no less true for Cyprus than it is for the Middle East or Northern Ireland or South Africa. To try in the absence of such commitments to intervene diplomatically would not only prove futile in the context of Cyprus but likely lead to major crises in American relations with Turkey, Greece, or both if the United States applied the kinds of pressure and threats that advocates of diplomatic activism favor (for example, cutting security assistance to Turkey). It is also far from certain that such pressure would work. Anti-Americanism and neutralism are sufficiently strong in both Greece and Turkey that one country or both could well reject the entreaties of the United States relating to Cyprus, even at significant cost to the larger relationship with the United States.

At the same time, holding back is not in itself a viable policy. It is not so much that a crisis is imminent—none appears to be —but rather that domestic politics in the United States, and more significantly relations with the alliance, demand that the United States become more involved. Simple drift could also harden the division between the island's two communities. This would not only make a future settlement even more difficult, but virtually guarantee a permanent friction in American relations with both Greece and Turkey and possibly set the stage for some desperate act that could trigger the first real crisis on the island since 1974.

As a result, the United States should couple a posture of restraint vis-à-vis formal negotiations with a more active private and public diplomacy. This would make clear that the status quo is less than desirable and that reunification is in the interests of all concerned, that reasonable formulas exist for resolving the Cyprus dispute, that the responsibility for progress rests largely with the Greeks and Turks themselves, and that all parties should avoid steps that would exacerbate tensions and possibly trigger a crisis; among these are reinforcing military presences, building settlements on disputed lands, or refusing to work with United Nations peacekeeping forces.

To complement this set of themes, the United States should work to ensure the continued presence of the United Nations peacekeeping force in Cyprus (UNFICYP), which comprises two thousand troops from seven nations. Formed in 1964, this force mans the green line and separates the two communities and their armed forces, as well as those of Greece and Turkey that are on the island. The countries that contribute troops are reportedly restless over the lack of progress, but their mission should be viewed as a success if peace is maintained. In this vein, Washington should discourage the notion sometimes expressed on the island that another crisis or outbreak of violence would somehow shock the United States and others into a more activist diplomatic posture. War in 1974 failed to stimulate political compromise; there is no reason to think a new outbreak of fighting would have a different result.

The United States should resist promoting new, grand diplomatic initiatives by the United Nations or other third parties. Although the United States will find itself hard put not to lend diplomatic support to any renewed effort of the United Nations secretary-general, there is much to be said for holding off new efforts until significant numbers of Greek Cypriots and Turkish Cypriots as well as the governments of Greece and Turkey demonstrate a greater willingness to solve their own problems. Premature negotiation—negotiation in the absence of ripeness—is likely only to provide justifications for steps that would make the island's division more permanent and possibly bring about a crisis.

The United States should also make available financial aid that could be drawn on to finance specific projects contributing to the peaceful reunification of Cyprus. Aid could also be used to reward steps taken in the same direction. (A contingency fund of $250 million for this purpose was created by the Congress in 1984 at the behest of the Reagan administration.) More generally, outsiders should promote and where applicable offer to fund a range of confidence-building measures: an all-Cyprus university, athletic teams, language instruction, environmental and health projects, economic development efforts, and so on. These would bring Greek Cypriots and Turkish Cypriots together and help reduce the mistrust that makes traditional diplomacy all but impossible.

Thus while supporting in principle the resumption of more formal diplomatic processes, the United States ought to champion a more informal process of normalization and confidence building. One useful stabilization measure was the "deconfrontation plan" advanced in May 1989 by the United Nations, according to which local militias stationed along the buffer zone of the United Nations were more clearly separated. Verifiable Turkish troop reductions should constitute an element of diplomacy, as should a relaxation by Greek Cypriots of their economic embargo of the North. Shortsightedness is being shown both by the Greek Cypriots, who oppose lifting the embargo or reopening the airport in Nicosia for fear that it will make the status quo too comfortable for the Turkish Cypriots, and by the Turkish Cypriots themselves, who oppose troop withdrawals and joint projects for fear of being overwhelmed by their more numerous Greek Cypriot neighbors. It is only through such confidence-building steps that another Cyprus crisis will be avoided and an environment will develop in which more traditional diplomacy can prosper.

It is unlikely that a near-term political solution will be brought about by these policies: expressing views of what should be done and what should be avoided, supporting extended multinational peacekeeping operations, forgoing formal negotiation until the local parties demonstrate a greater willingness to compromise, providing economic and political support for a regime of confidence building and sustaining opposition to steps that would make permanent the division of the island. But unfortunately the situation is not ripe for a political solution. Greeks and Turks, within Cyprus and without, remain unprepared for ambitious diplomacy. Something more ambitious ought to be contemplated only when Greeks and Turks, as well as Greek Cypriots and Turkish Cypriots, are prepared to make difficult compromises on issues of central import. Problems in international relations tend to get solved in one of two ways: through coercion or negotiation. No outside person or power can impose a settlement of the Cyprus problem (or for that matter the Aegean problem). Neither situation is yet ripe for negotiation, because the local leadership has not yet concluded that the status quo is less desirable that what could be agreed on through diplomacy, and that the political risk inherent in negotiating is either worth taking or unavoidable.

For now the only realistic task for the United States is one of management: to prevent a deterioration in the current situation and help to bring about circumstances in which diplomatic progress could occur. The United States should also concentrate on improving its bilateral relations with Greece and Turkey, and not allow them to become hostage to differences between the two countries. Confidence-building measures can help promote regional stability, and making the provision of aid conditional on specified actions may help improve bilateral ties (so may the introduction of aid-related incentives, rather than just sanctions). But Americans must recognize that the eastern Mediterranean defies easy prescriptions; not until the local actors demonstrate a greater desire than the United States does to solve their own problems are the diplomatic efforts of anyone else likely to bear fruit.

# 4

## INDIA AND PAKISTAN

As in the case of Israel and its Arab neighbors, or of Greece and Turkey, American attempts to fashion close, friendly relations with India and Pakistan have been a staple of American foreign policy since the late 1940s. And as in these other cases, the attempts have fallen short in two key ways: Washington has been unable to institutionalize a peace between the region's principal powers, and in the process its bilateral relationship with each has suffered.

South Asia, defined here, somewhat narrowly, as India and Pakistan, is more important than many observers appreciate. This is due not only to the size of the populations and the volume of trade and investment, although these should not be overlooked. South Asia is now a region of great potential danger. In 1987 alone there were near crises along India's borders with Pakistan (in late January and early February, and again in September along the Siachen Glacier, in Kashmir) and China (in May). Four of the world's principal military powers—the United States, the Soviet Union, the People's Republic of China, and India—interact in the region, with some friction. Any local conflict between India and Pakistan or between India and China could escalate with the involvement of the superpowers. South Asia could become in the late twentieth century or the early twenty-first what the Balkans were in 1914, when the great powers were drawn into direct conflict by their respective client states and associates. Even more serious is the technological potential of India and Pakistan to produce nuclear weapons: this adds another dimension to their rivalry, one that could bring about a limited but still devastating nuclear conflict and again risk involving the great powers.

## From Truman to Reagan

For much of the postwar period the United States has managed to limit its involvement in South Asia. American interests in this region were important but not vital. The United States sought to establish friendly ties both with the world's second most populous country (also the world's largest democracy) and with its neighbor Pakistan. India in particular was to be a model of successful noncommunist economic and political development that other third-world nations would emulate. At the same time, the United States sought to contain the influence of the Soviets and even more the Chinese; the Sino-Indian conflict of 1982 only heightened American concerns over the intentions of Communist China. To further these ends the United States drew Pakistan into a series of multilateral and bilateral security arrangements (nonaligned India would have no part of them), and provided to both countries modest military assistance and massive economic assistance.

By the mid-1960s, however, American policy was forced to accommodate new realities. Traditional enmity between largely Hindu India and Muslim Pakistan spilled over during 1965 into fighting triggered by disputes over the contested region of Kashmir. Arms provided to India and Pakistan to contain communism were used for the more prosaic purpose of settling old scores. The United States therefore suspended military assistance to both countries after the war, an ostensibly evenhanded gesture that in fact hurt Pakistan far more given its almost total dependence on Washington for military material. (This reality did not improve the image of the United States in New Delhi, where anti-Americanism was strong owing to the decision of the United States to arm Pakistan in the first place.) The immediate result of the war and of the changed American policy resulting from it was a new opportunity for others to gain influence at the expense of the United States: the Soviet Union in India, the People's Republic of China in Pakistan.

In 1969 the new administration of Richard Nixon and his chief foreign policy adviser, Henry Kissinger, responded to the opportunities inherent in the changed regional and international picture. To begin with, the United States was heavily burdened and preoccupied with Vietnam; there was no appetite for increased engagement in another part of Asia. India was demoted in the eyes of the United States and no longer seen as the key third-world state, owing in part to its seemingly endemic internal problems, in part to its increasingly close ties to Moscow. And perhaps most important as an explanation of American policy, Kissinger and Nixon understood that the growing gap between Moscow and Peking provided the United States with the leverage it needed to improve its position vis-à-vis the Soviet Union, its principal adversary. Exploiting this tension required developing a relationship with a long isolated China, something both men were eager to do. In the process the politics of South Asia were forever changed; suddenly the United States perceived China as a useful influence in Pakistan to balance growing Soviet inroads in India. To close the loop, Pakistan became the chosen secret channel for developing relations with China.

The new approach was not without inherent limitations, however. War again came to South Asia in 1971, in this instance triggered by severe Pakistani repression in its eastern territories, a massive flight of refugees into India, and the intervention of the Indian army against Pakistan, purportedly to end the flow of refugees, but also to weaken Pakistan and establish Indian primacy on the subcontinent. This time China proved too weak a friend to Pakistan to do much more than protest. The United States, already overextended in Southeast Asia, did little more than dispatch a show of naval force after East Pakistan (soon to reemerge as Bangladesh) became detached from the rest of the country. This show of force was ostensibly related to the protection of

American nationals in the area but in truth was meant as a signal to India that it ought not move against what remained of Pakistan. The naval force may also have been intended as a signal to Peking of American support for its ally Pakistan and of its coolness toward the Soviet Union and its new ally India, which only months before had signed a bilateral treaty of "peace, friendship, and cooperation." But whatever the intention, the show of force proved too little and too late either to help or satisfy the Pakistanis, but large enough to confirm a perception of American hostility in India, which emerged from the conflict as South Asia's dominant power.[1]

Relations between India and Pakistan improved somewhat after the war of 1971. July 1972 marked the signing of the so-called Simla accord, the two signatories to which expressed a commitment to solving peacefully their outstanding problems, their opposition to the threat or use of force, and their respect for each other's territorial integrity. More specific provisions included the withdrawal of all troops to the borders prevailing before 1971 and the honoring of the cease-fire line of December 17, 1971, in both Jammu and Kashmir. The two also pledged to hold further talks regarding repatriation of prisoners of war and civilians, a final settlement to territorial disputes, the formation of economic, cultural, and scientific ties, and the restoration of diplomatic relations. Just over a year later, in August 1973, India agreed to the release of most of the ninety thousand Pakistani prisoners captured during the war. Here was an apparent case where war and its results improved or at least stabilized relations between traditional antagonists.[2]

Amid this relative calm, and much as was the case after the Kashmir conflict of 1965, the United States largely retreated from South Asia. Assistance remained at modest levels, although a one-time sale of arms to Pakistan in 1973 and the full lifting of the arms embargo to both countries in February 1975 allowed the United States to resume arms sales to the region and to Pakistan in particular. Protests by the United States against India's "peaceful nuclear explosion" in 1974 were perfunctory even though the test constituted a major failure of the nuclear nonproliferation regime and presaged a new round of political and military competition in the region. Except for a modest expansion of its naval presence in the Indian Ocean, the attention of the United States was mostly focused elsewhere: on the final throes of its involvement in Vietnam, on an unsettled Middle East, on fashioning détente in Europe and beyond, and on its rising stake in the security of the Persian Gulf (and in oil from the Gulf).

The Carter administration assumed office with a major commitment to halt the spread of nuclear weapons. Its chief concern was that the increasing availability of nuclear reactors and their associated materials and facilities created possibilities for diverting highly enriched uranium or plutonium to the manufacture of weapons. For understandable reasons South Asia was near the top of the administration's concerns, for India had already tested a nuclear device and Pakistan had potential grounds for following suit. That Pakistan refused like India to sign the Nuclear Non-Proliferation Treaty of 1970 and make all its nuclear facilities available to international inspection only exacerbated matters. Pakistan's acquisition of a capacity to enrich uranium far beyond levels needed to generate power led the Carter administration to terminate all security assistance. Pakistan was not dissuaded; to the contrary, Prime Minister Zulfikar Ali Bhutto declared his country's willingness to "eat grass" if necessary to catch up to its rival India in the nuclear sphere. India's mistrust of American policy lingered, and the influence of the United States in the region reached its nadir.

The Soviet invasion of Afghanistan on Christmas 1979 forced a reassessment of American policy toward South Asia. The American position in Iran had just disintegrated, and Pakistan assumed a new strategic significance. Not only were Afghan refugees streaming across the border, but Afghan resistance groups were using Pakistan as a staging area. A friendly, secure Pakistan was a necessity if the resistance were to have a chance to hold off the Soviets and their Afghan allies. The Carter administration, however, still emphasized nuclear nonproliferation, and its policy reassessment in 1980 led to offering Pakistan only modest assistance. Pakistan's new leader, President Zia ul-Haq, was not impressed. He dismissed the offer as "peanuts," clearly suggesting that the United States would have to offer much more aid if Pakistan were to be persuaded to risk provoking Moscow or to rethink its commitment to matching India's nuclear program. Nor was the possibility lost on Pakistan that a Republican successor to Jimmy Carter might be prepared to come up with a more generous offer.

The Reagan administration entered office intent on a new approach. Although it too sought to deflect Pakistan's desire to acquire nuclear weapons, it believed that it would be futile to deny aid until criteria were met governing the inspection of all nuclear facilities. The administration argued further that a relationship based on security assistance would give Pakistan an alternate route to security and in the process give leverage to the United States, its principal source of conventional weaponry. If push came to shove, the United States could always threaten to terminate the flow of aid; explicit threats were unnecessary, for the potential to cut off aid was embodied in laws governing American nonproliferation policy.

That said, the leverage worked in both directions. The United States did not have the luxury of terminating all aid to Pakistan without incurring real costs in the process; nonproliferation objectives had to compete with the strategic necessity to make the Soviets pay for their invasion and occupation of Afghanistan. This latter requirement was the more important in the eyes of the Reagan administration, and necessitated a strong, pro-Western Pakistan that would be willing to stand up to limited Soviet intimidation while allowing both refugees and the Afghan resistance to base themselves in Pakistan.

The Reagan administration sought to square the circle in Pakistan with a large, five-year aid program of $3.2 billion, designed to reassure Pakistan so that it would feel less need to turn to nuclear weapons for security from India while it stood up to the Soviet Union over Afghanistan. Several years later (by 1985) the administration sought also to square the larger South Asian circle by improving ties with India; in this case the vehicle was to be advanced technology, which India wanted for economic and military reasons and some forms of which only the United States could provide (such as computers and jet engines). Soviet attempts to improve relations with India's archrival, China (which gained momentum after Mikhail Gorbachev assumed power), provided the perfect backdrop.[3]

The policy met with some success.[4] American assistance enabled Pakistan to undertake some much needed modernization of its army and air force. Substantial aid also muted some of the anti-American sentiments encountered in the Pakistani military and throughout Pakistani society. Pakistan accepted millions of refugees and supported many activities on behalf of the Afghan resistance, funneling hundreds of millions of dollars to the guerrillas based within its borders. The Soviet Union was consequently unable to pacify Afghanistan and failed to realize its ostensible aim of being confident that it could leave it without seeing it taken over by a hostile Afghan government.

Meanwhile, the relations of the United States with India improved as well, and their increase in trade and investment came about as intended. There were high-level political contacts, including several meetings, first between Indira Gandhi and Ronald Reagan and then between Rajiv Gandhi and Reagan, followed in October 1986 by the first trip ever made to India by an American secretary of defense (Caspar Weinberger). An agreement in mid-1982 allowed France to supply uranium to India's Tarapur nuclear power plant, built by the United States, thereby removing a major irritant to India's relationship with the United States.[5] A formal military sales relationship was resumed in 1985. In the following year the United States announced that India could purchase the GE 404 engine needed to power its planned light combat aircraft; two years later, during Secretary of Defense Frank Carlucci's first trip to the region, it was announced that India would receive an advanced gyroscope needed for the same aircraft project.

This progress notwithstanding, the ability of the United States to deal effectively and simultaneously with each of these bitter antagonists has run up against sharp limits. The Indians resent that they are not eligible to receive the highest forms of American technology, which they are denied owing to fears by the United States that the technology might end up in Soviet hands (because of the close ties between New Delhi and Moscow), and more general concerns over whether it serves American interests to promote a more powerful India. For years the United States would not allow access either to F-20 fighter technology or to the Cray supercomputer. Although these particular problems were resolved, the more general issue remains. India wants nothing less than the state of the art; the Defense Department wants India to make do with technology that is somewhat less capable (but still formidable). Computer capacity is not the real issue. Like virtually everything else in this part of the world, the symbol, in this case the willingness of the United States to treat India as a trusted friend, quickly assumes greater importance than the substance.

Indians resent even more the high level of American military support for Pakistan. Explanations by Washington that the aid is provided in the context of the invasion of Afghanistan and not that of Indo-Pakistani rivalry carries little water in New Delhi, where similar words in the past did not prevent American arms from being used by Pakistan against Indian targets in times of local conflict. The renewal of Pakistani-American ties that followed the Soviet invasion of Afghanistan (and that resulted in Pakistan's military revival) is resented by New Delhi as again symbolizing Washington's refusal to accept Indian primacy in the area. The Reagan administration sought to assuage both countries by offering Pakistan capable arms, though not the most advanced ones available. Typical was the attempt to provide Pakistan with an airborne warning and control system (AWACS). India opposed any sale, arguing that it was unnecessary to meet the alleged threat to Pakistan posed by Soviet aircraft based in Afghanistan, and that the system would only be used by Pakistan in some future war with India. Pakistan meanwhile wanted only the most advanced American system, akin to the one used by NATO. The United States tried to split the difference, offering the Pakistanis an intermediate AWACS. Not surprisingly, this offer was received poorly both in Islamabad for being too little and in New Delhi for being too much.

At the core of the region's instability (and Washington's dilemma) is the enduring mistrust between India and Pakistan, which has several sources. Perhaps most basic is the traditional religious and ethnic rivalry between mostly Hindu India and Muslim Pakistan. This rivalry is exacerbated by India's resentment of Muslim Pakistan's very existence (owing to India's viewing itself as a secular state that obviates a separate Muslim one) and Pakistan's unease with the apparent loyalty of some of India's ninety million Muslims to New Delhi rather than to Islamabad. The "divide and conquer" legacy of colonial rule and the hasty British departure after the close of World War II left little time for normal relations to develop. Enduring territorial disputes are both a cause and a reflection of this mistrust. And the inequality in size and strength between the two countries is a source of instability, in that Pakistan refuses to accept Indian primacy and India refuses to accept anything else.

Reinforcing the concerns of India and Pakistan over each other's intentions is the periodic outbreak of heightened tensions between these two old rivals. The most recent dangerous crisis came in early 1987, when a large Indian military exercise in the border state of Rajasthan (Operation Brass Tacks), near the Punjab, led Pakistan to undertake its own mobilization. Last-minute diplomacy that resulted in a mutual stand-down from the common border averted only narrowly yet another South Asian war (the fourth if one includes the strife that occasioned the end of British rule in the subcontinent and the conflicts of 1965 and 1971).

In such circumstances it is tempting to turn to traditional diplomacy. Suggesting that India and Pakistan intensify traditional diplomatic efforts to resolve their territorial disputes is always an option. Another is negotiations toward agreements placing quantitative or qualitative ceilings on armaments, either at existing levels or eventually at lower levels. In both instances the good offices of the United States or other third parties could be made available to India and Pakistan.

Yet these and related diplomatic measures are likely to have a limited impact. Traditional diplomacy, which often focuses implicitly on the root causes of disputes, would almost certainly fail. Territorial differences will likely continue to resist solution. More formal arms control, for example reductions in forces, is out of reach given that India harbors regional ambitions all around the Indian Ocean and in any case sizes its forces not simply against Pakistan but also against China. The atmosphere is poisoned by each country's fears that in an effort to distract and weaken its central government the other country is aiding and manipulating internal tensions (India believes Pakistan aids Sikh separatists, Pakistan believes India aids Sindhi separatists).[6] What all this does is ensure that a climate of mistrust and suspicion will continue to characterize Indo-Pakistani relations.[7]

The South Asian problem is unripe for solution, although Pakistan and India have regular consultations. On some issues, for example armament levels, there may be no formula that would satisfy both India (given its concern with China) and Pakistan (given its preoccupation with India), but for the most part what accounts for continuing disagreements is not an absence of reasonable formulas for compromise. This is especially so when it comes to territorial disputes, which by their nature tend to lend themselves to division and compromise. What explains better than anything else why tension persists in South Asia is the rivalry and mistrust that form the core of the Indo-Pakistani relationship. As is the case in the Soviet-American relationship, it is the legacy of conflict and the physical capacity for future confrontation that more than any set of particulars combine to fuel the South Asian dispute. Reinforcing this mistrust from Pakistan's vantage point is an image of an increasingly interventionist India that reserves for itself the right to exercise power throughout the region.[8] No formula or negotiation can put such suspicions to rest. At the same time there is little sense of urgency, for the status quo is relatively stable and both governments have their hands full with domestic and international issues that cannot be put off. Therefore neither leadership has an incentive to confront such emotional national issues, which would involve real political costs, without promising returns that would justify the risk taking.

More likely to serve a constructive purpose would be a series of confidence-building measures. India and Pakistan could limit the size, number, and locale of military exercises, provide to one another either directly or through some third party advance notification of exercises, and arrange for the exchange of observers so that each could confirm the activities of the other. Demilitarizing contested border regions would contribute to stability. So too would cooperative arrangements in the area of law enforcement, which would be a bulwark against the interference of each nation in the other's domestic political arrangements. None of these steps would actually affect capabilities or solve core problems, but all if adopted would reduce tensions and the likelihood of an incident triggering a larger conflict.

## The Nuclear Cloud

Complicating matters severely is the nuclear issue. More than anything else, it is the nuclear dimension of South Asian competition that argues against the United States returning to the posture toward South Asia that it maintained before the Soviet invasion of Afghanistan, one that might be termed benign neglect (or in some quarters malign neglect). This is nothing new.[9] The Reagan administration's security assistance program to Pakistan was allowed to proceed only after Congress waived the Symington amendment, which forbids aid to countries importing unsafeguarded enrichment materials or technology unless the president ascertains that providing aid is in the national interest. Yet the five-year aid program of $3.2 billion begun in 1982 did not tempt Pakistan to get out of the nuclear business; there is ample evidence that Pakistan has continued to seek and develop technology used to produce weapons-grade uranium and explosive devices.[10] Pakistan refuses to sign the Non-Proliferation Treaty and will not open its nuclear facilities to international inspection teams, which would certify that no nuclear fuel was being diverted to purposes that might include the building of weapons, unless India agrees to these same conditions. In March 1987 the head of Pakistan's Kahuta nuclear research facility was quoted as saying that his country was indeed producing weapons-grade uranium and possessed the bomb.[11] Although this statement was later denied, most experts believe that Pakistan does possess or is on the verge of developing a basic nuclear weapons capability.[12] The official position of the Pakistani government is that although it has the capability to build the bomb (and enrich uranium above levels required for peaceful uses) it has not done so and has no intentions to.[13]

There is however no proof that Pakistan has crossed the nuclear threshold; the Reagan administration certified that Pakistan "does not possess a nuclear explosive device" and that American aid "significantly" reduces the risk that it will acquire one.[14] The aid submission of 1986 was accompanied by a request that Congress waive the Symington amendment for all six years of the proposed new assistance program. Congress balked, agreeing in the end only to a two-year waiver. Congress also added a provision that the waiver be rescinded automatically should India accept international safeguards on its nuclear facilities. This expression of concern by Congress gave substance to warnings by the American ambassador to Islamabad and others in the administration that Pakistan was jeopardizing its relationship with the United States by its nuclear ambitions. Nevertheless, that the Pakistani-American relationship will not be able to free itself of the nuclear millstone is suggested by subsequent events: for example the arrest in July 1987 in Philadelphia of a person of Pakistani origin seeking to purchase and export to Pakistan a grade of steel used only for enrichment purposes—had his efforts succeeded they would have

triggered another provision of law requiring that aid be terminated (in this case the Solarz amendment).

The administration's certification of Pakistan's nuclear status
may have been technically correct, but it seems probable that the
aid program simply forced Pakistan's efforts to be more covert
than they would otherwise have been, leading Pakistan to simu-
late certain capabilities rather than test them, which would have
resulted in a mandatory cutoff of aid under the law. Pressures
from the United States may also have had the effect of slowing
the Pakistani effort, giving the government reasons to proceed
more slowly than technology would permit. In late 1987 the administration requested (and received in part) a six-year aid package of $4.02 billion beginning with fiscal year 1988 (from October
1, 1987). This may sustain Pakistan's support for American policy
toward Afghanistan or elicit some assistance in fighting the international drug trade or building bridges to Iran, but it is unlikely
to induce Islamabad to compromise significantly its nuclear
ambitions.[15] Long-standing fear of Indian capabilities and intentions, a desire for leadership within the Islamic world, and doubts
over the reliability of guarantees from the United States or anyone
else have combined to foster a mentality of going it alone and a
powerful lobby for the nuclear option in Pakistan. Going nuclear
appeals to many.

India, meanwhile, seeing Pakistan's conventional rearmament
as well as its nuclear efforts and ever mistrustful of China and for
that matter of both the United States and Soviet Union, has done
nothing to terminate its own development of technology needed
for a full-fledged nuclear weapons effort. India maintains a number of power and research reactors, facilities to produce heavy
water, and plant capable of reprocessing spent fuel and producing
plutonium. A large number of these facilities remain without
international safeguards. India also boasts a large scientific and
technical community of scientists able to carry out not only an
aggressive nuclear research program but also a modern space and
missile effort. Eliminating the nuclear dimension of South Asian
politics is not realistic. This too is a situation not ripe for solu-

tion. Like the problem of fundamental Indo-Pakistani tensions, this one does not lack forums or mechanisms. Indian and Pakistani leaders have discussed nuclear matters in the past, and could in the future. More difficult might be finding a precise formula, for nuclear weapons cannot be "disinvented." Scientific and technical expertise exists, and the potential to fabricate weapons and delivery systems cannot be done away with. Nuclear disarmament may not be a realistic option.

But an even larger obstacle to eliminating the nuclear dimension of the region's politics may stem from national perceptions. Indian leaders see no reason to renounce the nuclear option so long as China maintains a capability and the other nuclear powers have large arsenals. It is not at all clear that an Indian leader who thought otherwise could retain power. Similarly, there is no firm evidence that any Pakistani leader who wanted to close off Pakistan's nuclear future could prevail, because of India's capacity, doubts about the dependability of the United States, and strong internal pressures to retain the nuclear option. It is too soon to know whether such a route will even be pursued by Benazir Bhutto, who became prime minister in December 1988, some four months after President Zia died in a plane crash of undetermined causes. But there are grounds to doubt that she could renounce the nuclear option even if she wanted to in the absence of an Indian decision to follow suit.

We are thus close to entering a new era in South Asia, one that may well have far-reaching consequences for the region and the world. Before long South Asia could be home to two countries with a limited nuclear weapons capability. At a minimum, each country almost certainly has accumulated a sizable amount of fissile material (highly enriched uranium or plutonium) and either possesses or can produce on short notice a number of nuclear weapons that could be delivered by manned aircraft of the type already found in its inventory. With time, and even without full-scale testing of warheads, the number and efficiency of the weapons should increase and alternative delivery systems should become available (including surface-to-surface missiles), either from domestic development or from importation. (India tested its own medium-range ballistic missile, the "Agni," in May 1989.) Proliferation is better understood as a process than as an event. And the process of gradual nuclear proliferation, or nuclear creep, is well under way in South Asia.

A nuclear future would be fraught with danger. India, for example, might choose to attack Pakistan's nuclear facilities before it faced what it considered a real threat. Such an attack could be carried out by India using existing, nonnuclear military capabilities, and occur during a crisis or larger war or as an isolated event—much as when Israel attacked Iraq's nuclear reactor in the early 1980s. Even if the region managed without major incident the transition to a situation where every nation had nuclear weapons, there is no assurance that the result would prove stable. In part this danger is technical: although both India and Pakistan have a number of advanced aircraft with a large range, and despite India's impressive strides in developing a space and missile program, each country is far from having what would be described as a stable or mature retaliatory capability. By contrast, a vulnerable nuclear force would invite preemption. In part the issue is political as well, in that leaders and populations in this part of the world lack the experience of having nuclear weapons in their arsenals, and some would say they have not shown the ability to handle them responsibly. That both India and Pakistan have experienced difficulties in sustaining democracy and face separatist challenges only raises additional doubts about their capacity to manage successfully a balance that includes nuclear weapons.

Others, however, take a more sanguine view of the prospect of proliferation in South Asia. They believe that Indo-Pakistani relations have evolved positively since 1971, and that the chance of major conflict is remote; they also challenge the premise behind American nonproliferation policy, namely that having nuclear weapons in more hands only increases the likelihood these awful weapons will one day be used. Instead they argue that the technical requirements for stable deterrence are well within the reach of both countries, and that once stable deterrence were achieved it would be as effective as it has in the Soviet-American relationship, in which not only nuclear war but all direct conflict has been avoided for more than forty years. They also take issue with the notion that the leaders of India and Pakistan would act any less responsibly than their Soviet and American counterparts if they came to possess nuclear weapons.[16]

This more optimistic view of things may turn out to be correct, but there is little reason to assume that it will. It is impossible to predict the impact of moving toward or having a world of regional nuclear capacity. There is cause for concern, as there always is in uncharted waters, and owing also to the enormous costs of failure—a breakdown of deterrence. The transitional phase in particular poses great risks—that is, the years during which the two countries would have a nuclear capability of uncertain reliability and survivability. What is certain at a minimum is that any resulting conflict would not only bring great devastation to the region but raise the danger of catalytic war, of a broader conflict involving the United States, the Soviet Union, and China.

For the United States the approach to South Asia's nuclear reality must be twofold. For now it must work to freeze the status quo and prevent the emergence of a South Asia in which both India and Pakistan decide to build nuclear weapons. But if the two countries do accumulate sufficient fissile material, bomb casings, and delivery systems to have nuclear capabilities that are threatening but still vulnerable (a situation that would invite preemption or first use), the United States should seek to make these capabilities more mature and the nuclear relationship more stable. The central question for the United States becomes when to shift from a policy that emphasizes preventing the acquisition of capabilities to another that emphasizes preventing the use of capabilities already in hand.

So long as Pakistan's bomb remains either potential or hidden the United States can continue to finesse the problem. It should continue to provide security assistance to Islamabad, which can be a military and economic disincentive to go nuclear, even though it is unlikely to induce Pakistan to terminate its nuclear program.

But although the United States is unlikely to buy Pakistan out of the nuclear business with aid, neither should it extend a security guarantee to Pakistan—in effect placing Pakistan under the American nuclear umbrella. Pakistan would place little credence in any American guarantee, but one would nevertheless be enough to alienate India. Such a commitment would also prove impossible to make, much less meet. Congress and the American people would oppose it, the American military would deny having the resources to enforce it, and diplomats would find it unwise given all the disputes between India and Pakistan that could embroil the United States.

Again there would be a place for confidence-building measures, beyond those to reduce the chances of a conventional conflict that could bring about a nuclear conflict. The agreement signed by Prime Ministers Benazir Bhutto and Rajiv Gandhi on December 31, 1988, in which Pakistan and India pledge "to refrain from undertaking, encouraging, or participating indirectly or directly in any action aimed at causing the destruction or damage to any [nuclear] installations or facilities in the other country," is one such step.[17] Additional measures could include an agreement to declare the region a nuclear weapons–free zone (NWFZ), an agreement not to test nuclear weapons, observation by each country of the other's designated nuclear installations, simultaneous acceptance of the Non-Proliferation Treaty—all are at least worthy of consideration. And more traditional arms control can also be proposed, such as limits on potential delivery systems.

Unfortunately, none of these confidence-building measures is a panacea. India is likely to oppose most bilateral undertakings with Pakistan, owing in part to its concern with China, in part to a refusal to accord Pakistan a sense of equality. Pakistan is also likely to resist many such agreements. A no-testing pact would leave India the only state in the immediate region to have tested a device, and the scientific establishments in both countries are sure to want to continue developing and refining nuclear options. The agreement of 1985 between Zia and Rajiv Gandhi not to attack each other's nuclear facilities is instructive. A signature did not come for three years, a victim not only of mutual suspicions but of contrasting strategies. India seeks a modest upgrading of cultural, trade, and consular ties to Pakistan but is suspicious of grand nonaggression pacts. Pakistan meanwhile desires the symbolic equality implicit in such pacts but fears being overwhelmed by India should contacts and exchanges between the two countries take off. The best choice is confidence-building measures not directly concerned with nuclear issues but still able to prevent crises involving nuclear forces—for example advance notice of exercises, limits on the size and location of exercises, and special communications links.

But if Pakistan ever tests a nuclear device, or if its possession of a nuclear weapon is in some other way confirmed, the United States may want to change direction in its policy. The choice will be whether to introduce threatened sanctions or accept what has happened and work to manage the new status quo. Not many would agree with the latter notion. In such circumstances the United States (with Congress probably taking the lead) might find itself tempted to terminate or drastically reduce its aid to Pakistan. With the Soviet Union having withdrawn from Afghanistan, even a democratic Pakistan might find itself with few defenders.

Yet this could well be the wrong way to act. A policy designed to prevent the use of weapons by those who had acquired them would probably require dropping any threats to cut off aid; the argument now used to defend the aid program—that it is in the interest of the United States to give Pakistan a nonnuclear option —would still apply once Pakistan had nuclear weapons. The alternative would be to have Pakistan caught between certain conventional military defeat and the use of nuclear weapons—a situation reminiscent of NATO's posture of "massive retaliation" during the 1950s.

Under such circumstances the United States would probably want to work with Pakistan and India to promote arms control and reinforce their command and control systems, so that accidental war could be avoided. This policy could even involve selectively enhancing their nuclear capabilities so that the capacity to retaliate were strengthened and mutual deterrence reinforced. The aim of the United States should be to avoid another parallel to August 1914, when nations mobilized their armies for fear of being left at a disadvantage: the unfortunate parallel would be a situation where India and Pakistan rushed to complete bombs in their basements. If proliferation cannot be prevented, then the focus of policy must shift to deterrence. This in turn could best be accomplished by having in place robust, secure forces.

The United States might also want to consider helping Pakistan and India to develop a verification regime, for the gap in South Asia between military capability and intelligence is dangerously wide. Technology could be made available to India and Pakistan selectively to enable them to keep a watch on each other, much as "national technical means of verification" are used to monitor Soviet-American arms accords. The United States might also promote an agreement in which each side would pledge not to be the first to use nuclear weapons (a no-first-use agreement), recognizing that such a confidence-building measure might not hold much appeal in Islamabad, where it is inconsistent with Pakistan's view of nuclear weapons not simply as a deterrent to India's but also as a way to compensate for India's nonnuclear advantages (much as in NATO's doctrine of flexible response, nuclear weapons and their possible first use are the best way to deter an attack of any kind by the Warsaw Pact).

Any administration would want to enlist the Soviet Union and China in efforts to prevent or manage the proliferation problem. Unilateral efforts make little sense and have even less chance of succeeding, for the Soviets have armed India, and China may have aided Pakistan's nuclear program. Further, India may accept certain measures only if they include the People's Republic of China, and participation by the Soviet Union in some system of verification could lend it the political coloration required if it were to meet with the approval of New Delhi.

If the United States moved to such a policy of coping with proliferation in South Asia, there would be no need to do so everywhere; in other regions or with other countries it could persist in its nonproliferation efforts. Nonproliferation need not be seen as a seamless web. The notion that "we are compromised everywhere if we compromise anywhere" lacks foundation. Individual countries or pairs of countries are motivated to consider developing nuclear weapons mostly by immediate circumstance rather than by distant precedents. And in light of its support for the United Kingdom's nuclear policy and its de facto acceptance of Israel's, it can be argued that the United States long ago replaced a global policy of nonproliferation with one that discriminates along national and regional lines.

Gaining political support for a policy of management and discrimination would be extremely difficult, and no administration would take on the challenge unless faced with no alternative. Nor is there any guarantee that such a policy would succeed. The uncertainties and risks of a nuclear South Asia justify the efforts of the United States to prevent it. An active nonproliferation policy is a must: one mixing technical denial and security assistance, with warnings that the latter cannot be sustained if Pakistan violates certain nuclear norms. In addition, the agreement of April 1987 by the United States, Japan, and five European countries not to export large missiles (defined as capable of carrying a 1,100-pound warhead more than 190 miles) is a useful complement, although it is increasingly evident that ballistic missiles will proliferate as a result of domestic development and importing.[18] Again, measures designed to build confidence are likely to be both necessary and desirable: for example, advance notice of missile flight tests and no-first-use accords.

Even the best efforts of the United States are unlikely to eliminate the competition and potential for conflict between India and Pakistan. For better or worse, the two nations are a laboratory for a new phase of regional competition. What will make South Asia unique, and uniquely dangerous, is the nuclear dimension of the competition. Probably no amount of American activism will prevent the nuclearization of South Asia, which to a large extent is already a fact. The region is simply unripe for any such resolution. As in the Middle East and other parts of the world dominated by pairs of antagonists, a realistic goal for American foreign policy could well be to manage a seemingly intractable feud, to preserve regional stability, and to sustain a working relationship with each side. The United States should consider itself fortunate in the extreme if it succeeds.

# 5

## SOUTH AFRICA

South Africa offers a unique environment in which to examine the importance of ripeness. Unlike the eastern Mediterranean and South Asia, which are regions of conflict among nation-states, and the Middle East, which is marked by conflict among states as well as within Israel, South Africa is the focus of a conflict that is almost entirely internal. The conflict is also more controversial, for it is racial.

The politics of apartheid are an affront to most Americans, who rejected slavery, embraced the principle of one man, one vote, and built a legacy of civil rights. Yet while opposition to apartheid constitutes a general preference, it does not constitute a policy. Nor is it a substitute for analysis, for more than race and color animate South Africa's politics. More than many observers appreciate, South Africa has changed since P. W. Botha in 1978 succeeded John Vorster, whose government was plagued by scandal. A good deal of petty, or social, apartheid has disappeared, especially in the more cosmopolitan areas around Cape Town and Johannesburg. There are no longer laws prohibiting sexual relations and marriage between races, and regulations governing the movement of nonwhites (the so-called influx controls, or pass laws) have largely been eliminated.

But significant exceptions to the trend toward desegregation remain, and efforts to reintroduce social apartheid are gaining ground. Education (except at the university level) is still almost entirely racially organized, as is the health care system. Two pillars of apartheid remain as well. The first, the Group Areas Act

(1950), which assigns South Africa's whites, blacks, Coloureds, and Asians (mostly Indians) to separate neighborhoods, still prescribes housing options for most South Africans (or, more accurately, proscribes them). Even more important is the Population Registration Act (also 1950), which divides all South Africans into four racial and ethnic groups; this division constitutes the foundation of political apartheid. Meaningful political power is limited to the 4.8 million whites. The constitution of 1983 creating two additional parliamentary chambers for South Africa's four million Coloureds and Indians has provided these two groups participation without power. The approximately twenty-five million blacks who are South Africa's majority have no franchise or representation at all.

It was the hope of P. W. Botha and those around him in the ruling National party that these reforms would provide enough to satisfy South Africa's nonwhites and placate the outside world, all without significantly altering South Africa's political, economic, and social systems. The goal was to avoid alienating a majority of whites and above all Afrikaners, the descendants of seventeenth-century Dutch, German, and Huguenot settlers who today account for some 60 percent of all white South Africans. Botha miscalculated, however. Most Indians and Coloureds did not align themselves with the establishment, despite the ability of their new representatives to increase the flow of federal funds into needed public works and community development projects. Meanwhile, a large portion of the black community grew politicized, and violence increased markedly. More than two thousand blacks lost their lives between 1984 and mid-1986, mostly in the black townships. The outside world reacted to developments in South Africa with disgust, sanctions, and disinvestment. And conservative Afrikaners deserted the National party (NP), forming a second party to its right as well as lending support to the neofascist Afrikaner Resistance Movement (AWB). Botha's reforms proved too little for the politically disenfranchised to his left, too much for the reactionary forces to his right.[1]

The government implicitly acknowledged the failure of its reform attempts by proclaiming a state of emergency in June 1986. Botha sought to capitalize on the fear of violence and the bitterness over sanctions and disinvestment by calling for a special election to be held in May 1987 in which only whites could vote. He also sought a belated demonstration of approval of his tenure. What he received, however, was something less. After months of delay and debate, the election focused little on the past; nor did candidates spend much time attacking meddling foreigners or debating pocketbook concerns. The election turned out instead to be mostly a referendum on the future direction and pace of domestic political reform.

Although Botha's ruling NP garnered just over half of the 2.1 million ballots cast (some two-thirds of the 3.1 million eligible whites voted), and increased its share of the 166 elected parliamentary seats contested from 118 to 123, its percentage of the white vote fell, from 57 percent in 1981 to 52 percent, as did its percentage of the Afrikaner vote. The principal beneficiary of the election was the Conservative party (CP), which increased both its share of the popular vote since the last election (from under 20 percent to nearly 30) and its parliamentary strength (from seventeen to twenty-two). In the process the CP emerged not only as the only party to the right of the NP with parliamentary representation—the rival Herstigte (Reconstituted) National party lost its only seat—but also as the official opposition.[2]

The big losers in the polls were the left-of-center Progressive Federalist party (PFP), which saw its share of the popular vote fall by more than 10 percent and its parliamentary representation drop from twenty-six to nineteen, and its sister New Republic party (NRP), down from five seats to one. Three independent candidates, representing a center-left, reformist program, fared well in the popular vote, although the only one to win a seat was a former member of Parliament from the National party, Wynand Malan. Overall, the election is notable for the rightward shift of Afrikaners, 40 percent of whom voted for one of the two right-wing parties, and of the English-speaking whites, more than half of whom voted for the NP. More than 80 percent of whites voting chose either the conservative N P or one of the two far-right parties. Appeals to "security," often little more than an attempt to exploit whites' fears of violence and of black political power, had a dramatic impact. Subsequent political developments confirm these trends, at the same time underlining the absence of consensus in South Africa's dominant polity. In the whites-only election of September 1989, the Conservative party increased its parliamentary bloc from 22 to 39. The N P received less than half the popular vote, falling from 123 to 93 seats; the proreform Democratic party won 33 seats. Many questions about South Africa's future remain. Neither election produced a consensus on the country's future, on where it is going and how it will get there. Four visions of the future compete: majority rule, pervasive apartheid dominated by whites, power sharing, and white primacy with selective cooptation of nonwhites.

*Majority Rule.* The starkest alternative to the current political order is one that would eliminate the racial basis of political life and replace it with a color-blind system. Many refer to it as "one man, one vote," although there is no certainty that should political apartheid be overthrown it would result in democracy, multiracial or otherwise. Most advocates of such fundamental reform are black, although there are adherents among South Africa's three other racial groups. For many, such fundamental revision of political life in South Africa is associated with the African National Congress. This view is not without its problems, for the A N C's prominence internationally coincides with heightened uncertainty about its domestic capacities and prospects. Its executive is divided over tactics and objectives, and the communist representation in the executive ensures a struggle one day over the nature of the society that would replace the current one if the A N C ever achieved its goals.

Perhaps more important for the immediate future, the A N C's claim to represent South Africa's twenty-five million blacks is uncertain. The A N C is hampered by its illegal status and by the continued imprisonment of Nelson Mandela. The domestic political activities of the United Democratic Front (UDF), a loose-knit collection of more than five hundred organizations hewing closely to the ANC's line, are an imperfect substitute, especially after the government's order of February 1988 prohibiting the UDF and a number of related organizations from taking part in politics. The ostensible multiracial objectives of the ANC are not shared by rival black-consciousness groups, and its perceived patience and lack of radicalism are not shared by many of the younger militants. Increasingly, black townships, the homes of more than ten million blacks, are being run by street and community groups that pay only lip service to the ANC, which is often older and foreign-based. The burgeoning black trade union movement (more than one million blacks are now organized) is fast emerging as yet another source of political leadership. The ANC is in danger of becoming more a symbol of resistance than its core.

There is as well a more conservative alternative to the ANC in the black community. As many as one million blacks profess loyalty to Inkatha, a largely Zulu organization run by the KwaZulu chief minister, Mangosuthu Gatsha Buthelezi. The strength of Inkatha points up a more fundamental phenomenon, namely that tribal and regional factors continue to divide South Africa's blacks. So too do distinctions between the more urbanized, township blacks and those living in one of the more rural homelands. There is also a substantial and growing number of blacks serving in the police and armed forces.[3] And many blacks remain relatively unpoliticized and certainly nonradical. The violence in early 1988 in the city of Pietermaritzburg is but one indication of growing splits within the black population.

The immediate future is not bright for the advocates of revolution in South Africa. The ANC and UDF have been dealt a severe blow by the state of emergency. Some 23,000 people were imprisoned over the summer of 1986; thousands continue to languish. The police and the army did their homework, while leaders of the ANC and UDF seemed to ignore the crucial difference between mobilizing protest and organizing opposition. Press censorship continues to impede the flow of information, which would be necessary for mass political activity. Although the A N C does have the capacity to carry out sabotage against a wide range of targets, with only several hundred guerrillas operating within the country (out of several thousand poorly armed fighters overall) the A N C is not in a position to mount a military challenge to a government backed by a defense force numbering some one hundred thousand soldiers on active duty and another three hundred thousand on reserve.

*Rightist alternatives.* At the opposite end of the political spectrum are the true conservatives, or more precisely reactionaries, of South African politics. These are mostly Afrikaners who wish not only to sustain political apartheid but to restore social apartheid as well. They want to turn back the clock to 1948, when the National party of D. F. Malan upset the United party of Jan Smuts. They reject the reforms of P. W. Botha, arguing that they rather than the Nationalists now represent the true interests of Afrikaners and indeed all whites. The motto of these people, some still in the National party, most now in either the Conservative party (CP) or to a lesser extent the Herstigte (Reconstituted) National party (HNP), can be described as "one man, one vote, two societies." They fear the continued unraveling of social apartheid and the possibility that recent political reforms will only lead to black power. What they want is either a return to full social and political apartheid or a separate state consisting of traditional Afrikaner strongholds (the Transvaal, rich in mineral resources, the Orange Free State, northern Natal), with the rest of the country left to the blacks, Coloureds, and Indians. These two parties have going for them a certain logical consistency, namely their view that social apartheid should be protected by political apartheid. And they are animated by *swart gevaar,* the felt danger of being overrun by blacks in a continent often stifled by authoritarian and economically ruinous black rule.

Despite such consistency and strong showings in recent elections, the appeal of the Right remains limited. Its vision of restored apartheid is rejected by the majority of South Africans. For

blacks their policy resembles nothing so much as a glorified homelands policy, limiting blacks to the least desirable lands while
appropriating for whites the choice ones. Among whites, the English community distrusts the largely Afrikaner cast to rightist
politics, and business leaders believe that the approach of the cp
and hnp would only further isolate the country, in the process
denying it needed capital and technology. Over time, though, the
appeal of the Right may well increase, especially if violence
mounts and the National party continues to drift. In such circumstances the Conservative party could become the party of
government, or at a minimum pull the National party to the
right.

*Power sharing.* Power sharing in South Africa means different
things to different people. For some of its proponents, power sharing is intended as a transition to majority rule and one man, one
vote; others view a degree of power sharing as a permanent and
damage-limiting fix to South Africa's essential dilemma. Some
schemes emphasize the federal division between the central government and either states or provinces; others focus on the distribution of rights and powers within a particular level of government. In virtually every case, however, power sharing is intended
as a way of introducing black political participation in a form
acceptable to most blacks and whites.

What most if not all of the proposed arrangements have in
common is that they fall somewhere short of a pure arrangement
of one man, one vote (to reassure whites), while offering something other than a purely racial approach to politics (to satisfy
blacks). Black advocates of power sharing believe that half a loaf
is better than none and that by demanding all (as the anc does)
blacks will end up with nothing. There is also the more opportunistic consideration that those who participate will fare better
than those who do not. What motivates interested whites is a
desire to reach accommodation with blacks before it is too late,
and what gives confidence to many of them is the belief that
blacks will require whites to run South Africa long after blacks

acquire an interest in the political process, controlling or otherwise (much as has been the case in neighboring Zimbabwe).

The study and promotion of power-sharing schemes is now a cottage industry in South Africa, in which both government and private analysts are engaged. The author of a recent best-seller proposes to reorganize the country along the lines of Swiss cantons.[4] Other authors look to Malaysia or even farther afield. All are attempting to establish a political system that satisfies majority aspirations while safeguarding the minority.

Interest in power sharing is not limited to the government or academe. What many observers consider the most interesting political experiment of recent years in South Africa took place in the northeastern province of Natal, where leaders of the white community of Natal and their black KwaZulu counterparts (KwaZulu, one of the ten homelands, or "national states," is dispersed throughout Natal) have fashioned a constitutional blueprint along with Coloureds and Indians for sharing political power in a region encompassing one-quarter of all South Africans. The proposal known as the KwaNatal *indaba* (Zulu for meeting, or conference) would blend universal franchise (and hence majority rule) with extensive safeguards for the white minority.

Not at all surprisingly, the initiative came under attack from points all along the political spectrum. The UDF and ANC rejected the enterprise because of the central role of Chief Buthelezi (seen as little more than an Uncle Tom despite his having rejected "independence" for his homeland) and his Zulu-dominated Inkatha organization. The ANC also refused to countenance the provision for group rather than individual rights. And there is the simple fact that the effort constituted a threat to the ANC's own political prominence. The government and the leadership of the NP rejected the KwaNatal indaba on the grounds that the group safeguards were inadequate and the formulas for sharing power flawed. They found unacceptable that the proposed constitution only gives whites "protection against," not "provision for." The Afrikaner would be reduced to a negative blocking entity, no longer the creative force in his own land, and the government thus opposed the indaba as a precedent for the entire country, in large part owing to its substance, but also because it represents an act of political initiative sponsored neither by itself nor by the NP. Many Afrikaners found the appeal of it all further diluted because English speakers have traditionally dominated white participation. It remains to be seen whether this shortcoming can be overcome by the Democratic party, formed in April 1989 by former members of the PFP and Afrikaner independents. The strong showing of the Democrats in the election of September 1989 suggests some real potential. But not until power sharing is championed by the NP or by a large number of Afrikaners will it pose a serious challenge to the existing order or the government's own plans.

*Cooptation.* A fourth political plan for South Africa can be termed cooptation. Cooptation enjoys a strong tradition in contemporary South Africa; it is no exaggeration to describe it as the dominant feature of Afrikaner political culture. Unlike democracy, in which authority devolves from the bottom up and the leaders protect the interests of the people, Afrikaner politics begin with a mistrust of the individual and a subordination of the interests of the individual to those of the collective nation, the *volk*. Leaders dispense power from above; what results is not democracy in the Westminster or Jeffersonian sense but something much more directed. Afrikaners are not products of Europe's Enlightenment.

To perpetuate their rule, leaders of the National party have sought to coopt potential sources of opposition. Shortly after assuming power in 1948, the NP instituted a policy designed to end English domination. What ensued was a series of programs to uplift the Afrikaner to a level of equality; what resulted was a sort of Afrikaner affirmative action that created a new class of people beholden to the NP. The Afrikaner elite worked too to coopt the English-speaking whites. Sufficient privilege was ensured so that whites of all backgrounds would realize that their common interests outweighed any differences. In the early 1980s the NP sought to enlist Coloureds and Indians in the struggle against majority rule by offering them separate participation in Parliament and providing them with new resources to raise their standard of living. And in recent years the government has been careful to guarantee the support of the security forces, offering them as an inducement a greater voice in decision making.

Until recently cooptation had been applied to blacks in only an extremely limited fashion. To institutionalize social apartheid the NP embarked on a policy of promoting black allegiance to one of the ten designated tribal homelands. The attempt failed, however, as the homelands remained politically and economically unattractive to most blacks. Meanwhile, blacks continued to leave the homelands for often squalid living conditions on the fringes of metropolitan areas where jobs could be found. The government, though, maintained that these concentrations of urban blacks were temporary, and that blacks were citizens not of South Africa but of one of the homelands.

By 1985 even the NP's leadership had lost faith in its own fiction. Urban or township blacks numbered some ten million; there was no way they could ever be induced or even forced to return to the homelands. And the blacks were needed where they were, to provide labor to South African industry. They also represented a growing market for South Africa's own products. Last and most important, these urban blacks had come to dominate the politics of the black population; it was necessary to win them over, by carrot if possible but by stick if necessary.

A number of changes in policy followed. South African citizenship was restored to large numbers of blacks. Blacks as well as Indians and Coloureds were recruited for the security forces. Money is now being provided to build roads, housing, sewerage, and other basic services for the townships. Funds are being appropriated for black education. Legislation has been passed authorizing some twenty regional services councils that are intended to accelerate the flow of funds into black areas and possibly provide blacks with a limited form of political participation. In April 1988 President Botha suggested that blacks could come to participate in the electoral college and perhaps hold some positions of responsibility in the national government.

There will however be sharp limits to what is being held out. There is unlikely to be universal suffrage or a fourth parliamentary chamber for blacks—not even a powerless one. To allow either would create the possibility that the vote might lead to real political power. Treating blacks as a single entity would also contradict the tribal basis of Afrikaner politics. Pork-barrel politics run out of an Afrikaner equivalent of Tammany Hall are seen as the means of giving most South African blacks a stake in a minority-controlled political system. Meanwhile, the intelligence forces, army, and police will do their best to thwart the emergence in the townships of anything like the "people power" of the Philippines. The budget passed after the election of 1987 called for $4.1 billion to be spent over the next fiscal year on the police and military, a figure more than 30 percent higher than the preceding year's. And in the future security forces can count on ample funding, for the cabinet will continue to be steered by the State Security Council, a virtual shadow government led by the president but dominated by police, army, and intelligence leaders.

It is extremely doubtful whether any government dominated by whites can succeed in the politics of cooptation. Supporters argue that the state of emergency has set back the radical organizations and enabled different leadership to emerge. They believe that some prominent, moderate blacks can be persuaded to take part in white-dominated politics and thereby lend it some legitimacy. They note also that an unintended result of sanctions and disinvestment may be to stimulate South African economic activity, as local investors rush to fill the vacuum created by departing foreigners. Such growth, complemented by an increase in the price of gold, could provide the resources needed for a policy of cooptation.

The long-term prospects for cooptation are less promising. Although some blacks may be bought off, the majority may prove too politicized to remain passive indefinitely. Perhaps more important, few if any blacks with a substantial political following are likely to go along with token participation; so far, at least, influential blacks have resisted. (Turnout among black voters in the municipal elections of October 1988 was extremely low: around 10 percent of those eligible.)[5] Renewed violence is likely, possibly reaching white areas for the first time. The government is particularly vulnerable to outbursts inflamed by the excessive use of force by poorly trained police recruits. Economic growth could prove impossible to sustain if technology, capital, and markets were denied to South Africa. And over time, economic improvement among blacks in South Africa as elsewhere would bring with it demands for a meaningful political role. Therefore, cooptation contains the seeds of its own demise, even if it buys time for the white minority.

By this calculation cooptation becomes less a long-term policy than a holding operation. At some point the NP would have two options. Either it would have to halt the process of reform and be prepared to use increasing amounts of force to sustain itself, or it would have to allow reform to go considerably beyond what P. W. Botha deemed acceptable. The former would require reclaiming a traditional, largely Afrikaner constituency and in effect have the NP adopt much of the politics now espoused by the rightist parties; the latter would require reaching out to moderate and liberal Afrikaners and English to fashion a new coalition favoring real power sharing.[6] The limited power-sharing proposals articulated in June 1989 by the National party appear to constitute an attempt to bridge the two approaches. The problem for the National party is that the party lacks an independent ideology. Cooptation simply delays the day of reckoning.

## South Africa: Ripe or Not?

What may be the most important variable affecting South Africa's future is just how long cooptation can dominate South African politics. A long reign would provide time for many whites to accustom themselves to increased black economic and political power. It would also allow a relatively large black middle class to emerge. Both developments could prove crucial if a consensus were to emerge to replace apartheid with a working democracy. Because it is the Afrikaner establishment that holds most of the instruments of power, it will be the Afrikaners' unity that more than anything will determine the pace of change.

At first glance the world of the white South African and particularly of the Afrikaner is being buffeted as never before. Many observers inside the country and without are speaking of a *broedertwis*, a struggle among brothers, a crisis in Afrikanerdom. The synod of the Dutch Reformed Church in October 1986 reversed church policy on apartheid, declaring it not ordained by scripture and conditionally opening the church's doors to all regardless of color. Business leaders traveled to Lusaka to meet with the outlawed ANC executive; some sixty reform leaders, including a former head of the PFP (and an Afrikaner), Frederik van Zyl Slabbert, went to Senegal in July 1987 to meet with representatives of the ANC. White South Africans are resisting the military draft and leaving the country in noticeable numbers. Afrikaners associated with Stellenbosch University, a respected institution, are busy promoting a liberal alternative to the NP's current policy. As many as thirty members of Parliament belonging to the NP (or fewer owing to the rise of the Democratic party) may be "New Nats," proponents of dismantling large elements of apartheid. And the Broederbund, an officially secret political and cultural organization of leading Afrikaners that once functioned as a de facto steering group for South Africa, finds itself increasingly irrelevant, a victim of divisions among the Afrikaners.

The principal problem confronting reform-minded Afrikaners is that right-wing forces are growing in strength. A substantial number of white members of the Dutch Reformed Church are refusing to accept the synod's decision to desegregate; a small number broke off to form their own, segregated church in July 1987. The extraparliamentary AWB is able to attract a large following. Most important, the conservatives who left the NP in

1982 (and the HNP in 1969) fared much better than expected in the elections of May 1987 and in subsequent by-elections. Being the official opposition party will permit the CP to shape South Africa's political debate even more than before.

Should independent reformers (now the Democratic party) come to be stronger than they are at present, P.W. Botha's successor Frederick W. de Klerk could resume a limited reform process to satisfy his more liberal critics. He might, for example, provide for some black participation in the President's Council or the proposed National Statutory Council. By so doing he could claim to have taken into account the growing sentiment for power sharing. He also has the option of modifying or repealing the Group Areas Act, freeing Nelson Mandela from prison, or ending the state of emergency. In the foreseeable future, however, it is unlikely that much more than modest gestures will be made. The greatest challenge to the continued dominance of South Africa by the NP comes more from whites on the Right than from blacks on the Left.

More generally, the very real strengths of the Afrikaner establishment and to a lesser extent the National party ought not to be underestimated. Nearly half of all Afrikaners are on the public payroll, mostly as part of an enormous civil service bureaucracy, and are thus fearful of losing their jobs under a new government or political dispensation. South Africa also has one of the world's most highly regulated, statist economies (the government has been willing to pay an economic price for political control). And despite its cleavages the Dutch Reformed Church continues to exert a unifying influence. Defections notwithstanding, Afrikanerdom is not in imminent danger of breaking up. Most whites remain unaffected by violence and only marginally affected by the sluggish economic growth of the 1980s (about 1 percent a year). South Africa's whites, led by the Afrikaners, are digging in. Unlike the British, French, Portuguese, and white Rhodesians, Africa's "white tribe" believes it has nowhere to go.

The conclusion is clear: South Africa is far from ripe for negotiating away its internal differences in a manner that would be acceptable to a majority of its inhabitants. Formulas exist that would introduce substantial power sharing in a manner acceptable to all but the most radical nonwhites and protect the fundamental interests of the Afrikaner and English communities. Somewhat more of a problem is the question of process, but again there is no shortage of viable arrangements that either exist or could easily be created. The principal obstacle to negotiation in South Africa is rather the opposition to fundamental change on the part of most white South Africans. They have yet to conclude that the costs of sustaining the current state of affairs are unbearable. Making matters even more complicated are the political divisions within the minority, which increasingly are pulling the center of Afrikaner politics to the right. Violence, sanctions, and uncertainty are thus far making the situation less ripe for compromise rather than more.

But the impediments to progress are not to be found only in the white communities. Although the overwhelming majority of black South Africans favor dramatic change, there is no universally recognized leadership. Divisions persist: within the ANC, between the ANC and Inkatha, between black trade unions and other organizations. This makes it difficult for a moderate black political program to emerge and for a black interlocutor to step forward. The result is that both the majority and the minority are far from unified in support of a vision of South Africa that has any chance of being supported by most of the country's people.

## The American Role in South Africa

American policy toward South Africa has gone through several discernible phases of its own. The first and longest was characterized mostly by neglect; there was not even a separate bureau for African affairs under an assistant secretary of state until the 1960s. The attention of the United States was rarely focused on Africa, and when it was this tended to be because of a crisis (the Congo comes to mind) or for general humanitarian reasons. Other issues in Europe, Asia, Central America, and the Middle East took priority.

This pattern changed only marginally with the advent of the Nixon administration. A review of American policy in 1969 (outlined in National Security Study Memorandum 39) appeared to argue for the United States to associate itself more broadly with existing regimes in southern Africa, black and white alike, as the best means of fostering desired domestic change and resisting Soviet and Chinese encroachments in the area. In fact the study looked at five options: closer association with white regimes, broader and relatively even-handed association with both black and white regimes, a limited tilt toward the black regimes but with continued ties to the white regimes, dissociation from the white regimes, and dissociation from both black and white regimes. The second and third options seemed to be the most seriously considered, and ultimately the study favored the second. The result, though, was little change to policy.[7]

Calculations of the strategic balance between East and West dominated the administrations of Richard Nixon and Gerald Ford. This did not begin to change until the mid-1970s, although here it was not the situation in South Africa itself that concerned the United States but rather events in Angola, where after Portugal's revolution and withdrawal from Africa, forces supported by the United States and South Africa were defeated in a civil war by forces supported by the Soviet Union and Cuba. The most visible sign of new concern about the region came in a speech given in April 1976 by Henry Kissinger, in which he expressed the desire of the United States for a peaceful end to apartheid in South Africa.[8] This pronouncement was however not followed up in the less than one year that remained in the administration; what seemed to animate Kissinger's concern was less South Africa than southern Africa, and in particular the fear that what had happened in Angola might repeat itself in Rhodesia/Zimbabwe and Namibia if the United States and the West did nothing but stand by existing white regimes. Toward this end, the United States lent support to efforts by the United Kingdom to broker a transition toward majority rule in Rhodesia—support that was in part undermined by congressional action (the Byrd amendment) mandating the importation of Rhodesian chrome in contravention of international sanctions.

The new thrust in American policy that began to emerge in the last year of Ford's presidency was reinforced sharply by the Carter administration, which dedicated a great deal of diplomatic resources to southern Africa in general and above all to assisting the ultimately successful British effort in Rhodesia/Zimbabwe. (It is interesting that although Henry Kissinger fails to discuss American policy toward the region in the first two volumes of his memoirs, Cyrus Vance devotes several chapters of his own memoirs to the subject.) The successful repeal of the Byrd amendment in 1977 both symbolized and contributed to this new involvement.

Toward South Africa itself the Carter administration turned up the rhetoric critical of apartheid. The American ambassador to the United Nations, Andrew Young, played an important role in these efforts, but so did the president himself. Vice President Walter Mondale met with President John Vorster of South Africa and ostentatiously demanded reform. To back up the rhetoric, the administration placed an embargo on police and military equipment to South Africa, voted in favor of harsh resolutions at the United Nations, and urged American companies doing business in South Africa to abide by a code of conduct intended to alleviate the plight of blacks.[9] Although this may have improved the standing of the United States in much of Africa and with large elements of South Africa's black population, it seemed mostly to strengthen the hand of Afrikaner nationalists and of those in the NP who opposed meaningful reform.

The Reagan administration entered office with a very different notion of how to achieve domestic change in South Africa and, more importantly (from its vantage point), gain South Africa's support for its regional diplomacy. The administration sought independence for Namibia and the withdrawal of Cuban troops from Angola, in exchange for an end to American and South African support for the UNITA rebellion.[10] Implicit in this approach was the adoption of a more friendly (or less critical) stance toward South Africa. This approach may be succeeding outside South Africa, in settling the Namibian and Angolan conflicts. But despite Washington's making some modest gestures (such as relaxing controls on technology exports) and easing off pressures for domestic reform, constructive engagement failed to promote significant reform within South Africa.

The Reagan administration's efforts were soon overwhelmed by violence in South Africa, triggered by the government's decision in 1983 to extend a limited franchise to Indians and Coloureds but not to blacks. Scenes of South African violence became commonplace on American television. The issue of apartheid gained unprecedented salience in the United States, owing in large part to the efforts of religious, student, and black leaders in the United States. This politicization of the issue led to a congressional domination of American policy toward South Africa, characterized by sanctions and calls for disinvestment, and culminating in the passage in October 1986 of the Comprehensive Anti-Apartheid Act. Early in 1987 the Reagan administration sought to regain control of policy (and move the focus of the debate away from sanctions) by initiating a high-level dialogue with the African National Congress. Secretary of State George Shultz met with President Oliver Tambo of the ANC in January 1987. Shultz also articulated a new policy, which continued to eschew sanctions but forcibly voiced American opposition to apartheid and support for a democratic process leading to constitutional guarantees of basic human rights.[11]

This latest approach is unlikely to have much more of a near-term effect than earlier ones did on South African policy inside or beyond its borders. But the United States cannot simply wash its hands of the matter: South Africa remains an important and in some cases unique source of strategic materials for the United States,[12] and Pretoria is one of the keys to bringing about stability throughout southern Africa, including Angola. But even more compelling than any reason of diplomacy, minerals, or sea lanes may be the moral and political stake of the United States in helping to avoid a prolonged, violent struggle along racial lines, which would pose tragic choices for American society and American foreign policy.

Current congressional policy is almost certainly not the answer. More sanctions and disinvestment, although possibly useful as a symbol of American political preferences to both the South African government and the political opposition, will increase the misery of blacks while retarding the emergence of a black middle class inclined to support democracy and capitalism. Companies of which American multinationals have divested themselves and that have been bought up by white South Africans have ceased to observe the so-called Sullivan principles, which set standards for the treatment of nonwhite employees.[13] Economic sanctions are also likely to slow the growth of black economic power, quite possibly the best path available for realizing political power. Disinvestment has tended to push whites into the *laager* (a defensive posture similar to "circling the wagons"), thus reducing further the chance for meaningful political dialogue. South Africa's government and corporate interests have the capacity to minimize the effect of sanctions; the result of all this is that sanctions tend to hurt more those the United States seeks to help than those it wants to pressure. It is highly unlikely that sanctions will convince South Africa's whites that sustaining apartheid is too dear and that dramatic reform is the better path. Sanctions are at most a limited instrument for ripening the situation so that diplomacy might prosper.[14]

And embracing more radical measures would prove futile or counterproductive. Absolute economic sanctions cannot be organized; there are simply too many other international pariahs and opportunists for an embargo to be effective.[15] Political sanctions, such as the withdrawal of the American ambassador or even a cutting off of relations, would only dilute what little influence the United States does possess. Providing military aid to the ANC would polarize the situation further, add to the violence, and strengthen those on both sides who oppose compromise. American military aid to the ANC would also be an unlikely development, for many Americans would oppose it on the grounds that the ANC had poor democratic credentials, maintained ties to Moscow, and lacked clear support throughout the country.[16] Perhaps more telling than such traditional arguments would be that many Americans would not be prepared to assist a largely black movement in a violent war against millions of whites. An even more radical option, the deployment of military force (for example, an effort to close South Africa's ports led by the Soviet Union and approved by the United Nations General Assembly), would result in the economic and physical collapse of South Africa's neighbors long before it affected South Africa itself.

The United States and other external forces that seek change must also take into account South Africa's capacity to respond. In addition to making life far more miserable for the majority and particularly those advocating political change, Pretoria can also introduce countersanctions, in the process denying needed minerals to the United States. Last, there is the all but certain reality of South Africa's nuclear weapons capability, which could allow the government (however irrationally) to threaten to use nuclear weapons against a large invasion force or even a range of civilian targets if external pressure became so great that the regime's survival were placed in jeopardy.[17]

The United States faces a dilemma: how can it avoid sustaining apartheid, while working to increase the chances that change will come with a minimum of violence and result in a legitimate form of democracy? Although traditionalists may argue that the United States should use its diplomatic strength to solve the South African problem, history suggests sharp limits to the ability of foreign forces to influence developments in South Africa. The report in 1987 of the advisory committee to Secretary of State Shultz pulls no punches in making this point, noting that "the ability of any U.S. administration to induce, force, or ensure specific outcomes is limited . . . the United States lacks the economic or political leverage to compel the white government to end apartheid and negotiate with its opponents."[18]

This is not surprising. South Africa does not fit neatly into a political taxonomy. It is partly democratic (for the nearly 5 million whites) and partly totalitarian (in that an efficient and disciplined government denies meaningful political power to most citizens and controls a good deal of the society's economic and cultural activity). It can also be said to be partly authoritarian (despite the controls, a good deal of independent economic and unsanctioned political activity go on), but it is unlike other authoritarian systems in that political power is based not in a person or clique but in a homogenous, motivated ethnic group. And South Africa is not at a vulnerable point in its evolution. This quasi-corporate, friendly tyrant is far from being in a crisis, although a case can be made that a crisis (however distant) is more imaginable now than before. This said, diplomatic ripeness remains some ways off.

The United States should do several things. The government and private American organizations, from universities and corporations to foundations and churches, should contribute to the welfare and development of the black majority, especially in the areas of education and job training. This would have the near-term effect of improving the quality of life for millions of people in South Africa; at the same time it would make blacks more likely to espouse moderate political and economic policies, and therefore more likely to sustain a dialogue with whites and to convince them that political change is not something to be avoided at all costs. Second, the United States should engage in a dialogue not simply with the ANC but with a broad range of South African opposition forces, including more moderate black leaders. Again, the purpose would be to promote the emergence of a critical mass of black South Africans who support moderate policies (that is, who seek a gradual participation in politics leading to reasonable power-sharing formulas, which would have safeguards for minorities and be unlikely to alienate the powerful Afrikaner establishment). It is also important to discourage violence, a tool more likely to harden the attitudes of Afrikaners than to ripen the situation so that a dialogue can take place.

At the same time the United States must deal with the government in Pretoria and with Afrikanerdom. Publicly and privately, officially and unofficially, with speeches and with more traditional diplomacy, Americans must speak truth to power. It must work to encourage the N P and Botha's successors to open the political process and adopt a reformist path, one that rejects reactionary appeals to reinforce apartheid and moves past cooptation to providing meaningful political participation to nonwhites. There can be no ambiguity in the commitment of the United States to the establishment of a system of government acceptable to the majority of all South Africans.

In these dialogues with black and white South Africans, the United States should not simply insist on a major and immediate revamping of South Africa's political and social institutions. There could well be a role for more modest steps, both at the local or regional level and at the national level. These would provide blacks with more political power than they now have and enable both blacks and whites to experience first-hand that power sharing and political participation by blacks are not inconsistent with political and economic well-being for all. The United States is more likely to bring about the solutions it wants if it is willing to contemplate arrangements that may fall short of the ideal in the near term but at least establish useful precedents and build the trust and confidence that the parties need for the long term.

Last, the United States can pledge its resources and those of its allies to assist South Africa in building the country and improving the welfare of its citizens once legitimate political reform is effected. By so doing, it can make clear that peacemaking will be rewarded, and that South Africans regardless of color will benefit every day from a new, more just political order.

What emerges from this list of options is an overriding sense of modesty. So long as the establishment's resolve remains high, the pace and direction of reform will be a function more of internal dynamics than of external pressures and inducements. In South Africa more than in most places, it is important to keep in mind that although other countries can influence processes of political development, they can rarely if ever fine-tune them. History, culture, religion, personality, wealth, force, even chance—any or all of these may have more of an impact than the efforts of American officials and diplomats. It is unfortunate for South Africa that these factors tend to frustrate political progress. Few white South Africans believe the time is near when they must give up most of their political and economic power. To them the status quo is therefore far preferable to the alternatives. And the increasingly divided leadership of white South Africa lacks the ability to persuade the white populace to relinquish most of its privilege (even assuming that it has the desire to persuade them, which it does not).

To make matters worse, those blacks inclined to compromise lack the power to do so, whereas those who appear to have the power lack the inclination. Formulas for sharing power (which are plentiful) appeal as yet to only a small segment of either camp. This is unlikely to change until white leaders (especially Afrikaners) decide that the status quo is no longer tenable. This could result from the mounting costs of sustaining apartheid (less because of sanctions or violence than because of apartheid's own inefficiencies and absurdities) and from an increased confidence that the alternative need not be as bleak as is now commonly presumed. There would then be a need to make specific political arrangements; these would appeal to an interlocutor in the majority that could claim legitimacy, and insulate the process from radicals on both sides who could be counted on to attack any meaningful attempt at a settlement. Such a scenario will take time to develop; for the near future, the challenge is to cope with a South African reality unripe for much more than modest progress.

# 6

## NORTHERN IRELAND

Northern Ireland is the scene of one of the world's most enduring conflicts. It is bloody (more than 2,500 people have lost their lives in the last two decades as a direct result of the sectarian violence), and bloody-minded, in that on all sides of the political divide one encounters a stubbornness and determination that discourage those who are optimistic about what men and women of goodwill can solve.

The situation in Northern Ireland in many ways resembles that in Cyprus: a relatively small area is divided along lines that are largely ethnic and religious; a majority and a minority population coexist uneasily; important ties link each of the two populations to external motherlands; and there is a history of violence. There are important differences as well. Cyprus is an independent state, Northern Ireland is not. Cyprus is for the most part spared the violence that is part of daily existence in Northern Ireland. And whereas Cyprus now consists of two distinct, geographically defined groupings, Northern Ireland is a patchwork quilt of Catholic and Protestant communities and families, more like the Cyprus that existed before the war of 1974 than the Cyprus of today.

Nevertheless, the commonalities outweigh the differences, particularly if one views the situation from the vantage point of the United States. A powerful ethnic group, in this instance the Irish-Americans, regularly pressures the U.S. government to do something to promote political change. Private Americans channel funds and in some cases more direct support to the opponents.

And relations with an important NATO ally are affected, in this case, the United Kingdom. As a consequence the same question arises: what, if anything, should be done by the United States (or by someone else, in particular the British government) to promote a permanent political settlement that is accepted by the majority of the people and their leaders, regardless of what community they hail from?

## From 1921 to the Present

It is difficult and in the end somewhat arbitrary to select a date from which to tell the history of Northern Ireland. One could in principle go back hundreds of years, to King James I and his decision to "plant" large numbers of Scottish Presbyterians in the ancient county of Ulster. Equally, one could choose 1800, the year the Act of Union formally incorporated Ireland into the United Kingdom, much as was done earlier with Scotland and Wales. For the purposes of the contemporary observer, 1921 is the most appropriate date, for it was then that the Anglo-Irish war ended. The result was partition. In the south, the conflict ended with the creation of the Irish Free State (which in 1949 left the Commonwealth to become the Republic of Ireland). In the north, six counties of the original nine in what was Ulster chose to remain part of the United Kingdom. These six counties, which make up modern Northern Ireland, came to enjoy a considerable degree of political autonomy, as the British parliament at Westminster was only too happy to focus its energies elsewhere.

The British government of the time hoped that this arrangement—an independent and predominantly Catholic Ireland in the south, an autonomous and predominantly Protestant Ireland in the north—settled the Irish problem once and for all. This hope proved unfulfilled. The settlement of 1921 set the stage for the present conflict in Northern Ireland, where some one million Protestants and nearly six hundred thousand Catholics live side by side, always uneasily and often violently. Accounting for this tension requires going beyond simple religious differences and intolerance (one can usefully think of Northern Ireland in what amounts to tribal terms), although these divisions and the history they have helped engender are clearly at the heart of the problem. Relations between the two communities were often bedeviled by the Catholic's resentment of their second-class status, in particular their feeling (with a good deal of cause) that the North's distribution of political power and economic opportunity was unfairly skewed against the interests and welfare of the Catholic minority. The parliament of Northern Ireland at Stormont came to symbolize this unfair division, as Catholic "nationalists" increasingly boycotted proceedings dominated by Protestant "unionists" or "loyalists."[1]

By the late 1960s this resentment among Catholics took the form of widespread public protests—along the lines of the American civil rights movement—that in turn triggered counterprotests by the majority. Violence quickly followed. In late 1969 was formed a radical, violent group, the Provisional Irish Republican Army (PIRA), allegedly because the traditional IRA had failed to protect the Catholic population against Protestant paramilitary forces. The British army entered the North in 1969 to restore and maintain order, in large part to protect the Catholic minority. In March 1972 London took over all security functions and introduced direct rule from Westminster, ending the autonomy that the North had enjoyed since 1921. Direct rule with a large security presence was seen by successive British governments as far from ideal. Few in London wanted the responsibility, and the cost in lives and treasure was enormous (the British army has stationed upwards of ten thousand soldiers in the North for nearly two decades).

London has searched periodically for a way out of the morass that Northern Ireland has become. In particular, two major political initiatives have been undertaken in an attempt to relieve the political causes of the violence. After elections in June 1973 for a new assembly in Northern Ireland demonstrated support all across the North for moderate political voices, the first initiative came in December 1973, when representatives of Great Britain, Ireland, and Northern Ireland met at Sunningdale, England, and approved a British plan that promised to bring about new arrangements for governance in the North. The agreement provided for executive authority consisting solely of representatives of Northern Ireland, in which Catholics and Protestants would share political power. Also included in the agreement were proposals for a Council of Ireland, an advisory body to consist of ministers representing the British and Irish governments that would promote political and especially economic initiatives of common interest. It was hoped that the combination of the two dimensions—power sharing and an acknowledged role for Dublin—would meet the fundamental grievances of Catholics and therefore end their support for the Provisional IRA and its campaign of violence.

The British government miscalculated, however, in thinking that the problem in the North was largely one of Catholic discontent. Real as this was, it was only part of the problem. Clear warning came in the Westminster general elections of February 1974, in which eleven of the twelve seats from Northern Ireland were won by unionists opposed to power sharing. In less than half a year Sunningdale's executive was disbanded, a victim of a Protestant (loyalist) general strike that brought the entire province to a standstill. Behind this protest, led by Ian Paisley of the radical Democratic Unionist party, was a rejection by the majority of what they saw as an unfair provision of power to the minority, and above all their rejection of the introduction into the Northern Ireland dispute of Dublin.

The strike might well have been broken had the British government, then led by Prime Minister Harold Wilson, been willing to use force against the strikers. But the Labour government possessed a majority of only two votes, a political fact of life that reduced any propensity for assertive action on its part. To use force would have risked a revolt in Labour's own ranks or the opposition of the armed forces, either of which could have brought down the government. The result was that force was not employed, and the strike ended whatever chance existed for Sunningdale's power-sharing scheme.

It was more than a decade before another British government tried again. This time the government took a different tack, one that placed devolution and power sharing on the back burner. Priority was given instead to according the Irish Republic a special role in the future of the North. In a sense this new effort reversed the components of the Sunningdale agreement. It was predicated on the notion that agreement between London and Dublin would be easier to achieve and could in principle lead to more comprehensive arrangements for governing the North, and maybe even to a settlement of the problem itself.

The Anglo-Irish Agreement of 1985 was signed on November 15 at Hillsborough Castle by Prime Minister Margaret Thatcher and her Irish counterpart Garret Fitzgerald. This agreement gave Dublin an advisory role in the affairs of Northern Ireland relating to politics, security, and legal matters, with London retaining executive authority. The formation of an Intergovernmental Conference was a compromise for each side: London acknowledged that Dublin enjoyed a special role in the affairs of the North, and Dublin agreed that the North would remain British until a majority in Ulster voted otherwise (this was a real breakthrough—it was the first time any Irish government had accepted this constraint). It was hoped that the new role for Dublin would reassure the Catholics and especially the moderate Social Democratic and Labour party (SDLP), which London saw as the only real moderate alternative to the Provisional IRA, which was outlawed, and its legal political arm, Sinn Fein. The support of the SDLP for Hillsborough was thus essential if the Anglo-Irish Agreement were ever to have a chance (or if power sharing were to have one down the road). For its part, the SDLP made its support contingent on London's acceptance of a role for Dublin (lest it be seen as undermining the hopes for Irish unity).[2] The concern preoccupying London at the time was that allowing the situation to drift would only strengthen the hands of the radicals at the expense of the moderates.

The British also promoted the agreement for reasons that went beyond the internal politics of the province. London wished to placate Dublin to elicit its increased cooperation on security matters, in particular in efforts against IRA terrorists, who often escaped across the border into the Irish Republic. Similarly, a nod in this direction would prove useful in the campaign to convince the U.S. Congress and others that Britain was sincere in its desire to improve the lot of Catholics in Northern Ireland and that as a result Americans of Irish descent should cease providing support to the Provisional IRA. At the same time, Prime Minister Thatcher's government tried to avoid the error made at Sunningdale of appearing to consider only minority (nationalist) concerns. It was hoped that the pledge to protect majority rights (that no change in the North's legal status could come about unless approved by more than half its population) would effectively give the Protestants a veto and thus placate the unionists.

Again the government in London may have miscalculated. From the outset Hillsborough has had a difficult existence. As with Sunningdale, most of the opposition came from Protestants, whose political leaders were clearly upset at not having been consulted. (The British government decided that consultations would effectively have precluded an agreement forever.) Making things even worse from the local Protestant perspective is that the agreement provides no real role for Ulster: the loci of decision making largely moved to London and Dublin. The main concern of Protestant leaders, though, has been less procedural than substantive. Despite the promise of majority control by Northern Ireland over its own future and enhanced security cooperation between the United Kingdom and the Irish Republic (which should diminish the threat posed by the Provisional IRA), the agreement is opposed because it is seen as the beginning of the end, a step that will inevitably lead to a diminution of British rule and the incorporation of the North into the South. (That the Irish constitution refers explicitly to the goal of reunifying all of Ireland does not help matters.) In the process radical Protestant leaders have become stronger, and those more inclined to compromise and share power are barely visible.

Reaction on the Catholic side has been somewhat better. Although pleased with the formal recognition of Ireland's role in the affairs of the North, some moderate Catholics feel let down by the daily impact of the Anglo-Irish Agreement. In particular there is disappointment with the apparent lack of progress in how Catholics are being treated by the security forces (the Royal Ulster Constabulary and the Ulster Defense Regiment are largely Protestant forces) and by the judicial system. Radical Catholics, and the Provisional IRA in particular, oppose the accord as simply a device to make what is for them an unacceptable status quo more acceptable to the majority.

The question arises of whether the British government was correct even to try. The Anglo-Irish Agreement does at least add some stability to the current situation, and provide a framework for satisfying some of the political requirements of Dublin and of the more moderate Catholics. At the same time, a case can be made that bringing the Irish dimension of the Northern Ireland problem to the forefront was certain to alienate virtually the entire Protestant population, not simply the more irredentist. London might have done better to emphasize power sharing, for which support exists in both communities in the North. If this had proved impossible owing to nationalist demands for a visible Irish dimension to any initiative, London might have eschewed any formal proposal, instead working to introduce modest confidence-building measures that would improve day-to-day affairs while creating circumstances in which power sharing might succeed. Instead, by launching an ambitious effort at Hillsborough, the government may have increased tensions to the point where even such modest steps will have a difficult time gaining acceptance in Northern Ireland from either community.[3]

## Political Choices

A broad range of possible futures can be envisioned for Northern Ireland, ranging from the status quo to full independence, with just about every conceivable arrangement in between.

A review of the most important options is useful, if only to demonstrate again that what accounts for the failure of diplomacy is not necessarily a lack of imaginative thinking.[4]

*Union with Ireland.* This is the purely nationalist option, desired by the Provisional IRA and a good many Catholics in the North. The problem is that this option is opposed by a majority of those in the North, namely the Protestants and some Catholics, who fear it would only bring about Catholic domination. Short of major demographic change, union with Ireland could come about only by coercion, which is not a serious possibility given the presence of the British army and the strength of local police, army, and paramilitary forces. Further, the recent Anglo-Irish accord makes clear that such a change could only result from majority choice; the majority is not about to make the choice.

It is also not at all clear that this option enjoys widespread support in the South. Many in the Irish Republic fear that such an arrangement would only import Protestant terror into their country. In addition, a good many Catholic politicians believe that they have little in common with the radical elements of the Provisional IRA, who would prove to be no friends of Irish democracy. The status quo, with the British army in the North and all, may therefore be more attractive to many in the South than union.

One version of unification that would factor in the concerns of Catholics in the South and Protestants in the North would place the North under the sovereignty of Dublin, but extend to it a considerable degree of autonomy. (This was in fact one of the models put forth by the New Ireland Forum in the early 1980s, in which the major political parties of the Republic as well as the SDLP from the North took part.) Such a federal, or confederal, approach would still be unacceptable to almost all of Northern Ireland's Protestants, regardless of any provisions designed to reassure them that they would not come under "Rome rule" in important areas of their personal and political lives.

*Independence*. This approach can be understood as the radical version of home rule. It could result only from a unilateral declaration of independence (UDI), the same device used by Ian Smith in Rhodesia years ago. It would be resisted as it was then, in this case by London, which would not look kindly on such unauthorized secession, particularly one that might fan the flames of Scottish and Welsh devolution. Catholics throughout the North would resist the move, violence would increase markedly, and Dublin would demand that London put an end to the rebellion; because of geography, London in this instance would be in a position to do something about it. But even if London were not opposed to the idea, it is far from clear that an independent Ulster would be economically viable.

*Full integration with the United Kingdom*. This option would make permanent what is now seen as temporary, and make Northern Ireland as much a part of the United Kingdom as are Scotland and Wales. (That the country is formally called the United Kingdom of Great Britain and Northern Ireland shows that the status of Northern Ireland is different.) Few in what is the United Kingdom are eager to become any more embroiled in the political and economic woes of the North; in fact, there is virtually no enthusiasm on the part of the British government or the public for Britain's responsibilities in Northern Ireland. Nationalists in the North would oppose this option vehemently, as would any government in Dublin. It is not even clear that most Protestants in the North would support it, for they might prefer independence or a large dose of home rule to domination by Westminster.

*Repartition*. This approach would "solve" the problem of Northern Ireland by giving up on attempts to bring about harmony between Catholics and Protestants in the North. After some population movements, part of what is now the North (populated largely by Catholics) would join the South, and the remainder of the North (largely Protestant) could again receive home rule within the United Kingdom. An analogous formula in Cyprus would involve taking the configuration in effect after 1974 and then adding double enosis, joining the Greek Cypriot portion of the island to Greece and the northern, Turkish Cypriot part to Turkey.

This proposal for Northern Ireland also fails to hold up under scrutiny. Even assuming complete homogeneity within each community, which does not exist, there is no neat and easy way to separate Catholics from Protestants. Large shifts of families and communities would be required, and even then there would be exceptions to the "purity" of the zones. Nationalists would reject this approach as compromising the principle of a united Ireland; loyalists would again fear that this was only the thin end of the wedge and that it was only a matter of time before Dublin managed to incorporate all of the North.

*Condominium.* At the heart of the notion of condominium (in effect, the sharing of authority by outside powers) is a recognition that there is no precise formula for settling the problem of Northern Ireland so long as one thinks in terms of absolute sovereignty. The notion of condominium accepts that both Ireland and the United Kingdom have a stake in the North, and that none of the other options—in particular independence or union with the South—is politically viable. The approach is central to the Anglo-Irish accord of 1985; at least in principle, it could be applied to a North that is part of the United Kingdom (as it is now) or to a North that enjoys autonomy without sovereignty. As such, it closely resembles proposals put forth for the West Bank and Gaza, in which the territories now occupied by Israel would enjoy a degree of self-rule in association with Israel and Jordan (but not self-determination leading to sovereignty).

A condominium is an ingenious means to finesse the dilemma of sovereignty. But it too has its limits, both in general and in the context of Northern Ireland. It tends to be not enough for those who want radical change—in this case, the Catholic nationalists seeking union with Ireland—and too much for those who fear that any change to the status quo that increases Dublin's role will over time spell their doom (many Protestants and loyalists feel this way). What is at issue is not simply the principle of the idea but how it works in practice; as is often the case, the devil, and the difficulty, lie in the details.

*Power sharing*. Anglo-Irish condominium is one important dimension of the United Kingdom's current policy; power sharing is the other. What is desired is not simply a devolution of power to the North, but rather a sharing of devolved power, a qualified home rule. This concept was at the heart of Sunningdale, and constitutes what might be called the second tier of Hillsborough. The difficulty with power sharing, as with condominium, lies in its implementation, and in particular in how power is to be shared. Loyalists want to keep sharing to a minimum; moderate Catholics fear just that, and are skeptical that the majority will go along with anything more than token reforms. More radical nationalists are not only skeptical but opposed outright, fearful that successful power sharing would undermine support for their goal of unifying all of Ireland.

## Choices in Fact: The Consequences of a Lack of Ripeness

None of these so-called solutions is a real solution. It is not that they are worse than the status quo: several approaches in whole or in part would be better than the current situation, which costs many lives and hurts the quality of all lives. One can also design a host of political processes involving representatives of Dublin and London, as well as the two communities in the North. But for a number of reasons such arrangements are beyond reach. The situation is simply not ripe for anything beyond the most modest achievements.

Why this is the case deserves examination. In both the Protestant and Catholic communities are powerful elements that resist compromise. Many nationalists are unwilling to accept anything less than union with Ireland, preferring to fight for this total objective rather than accept something that might be better than the current situation but still less than the ideal one. At the same time many loyalists oppose the sorts of halfway measures—power sharing and condominium—that might appeal to moderate Catholics, for fear that it would lead over time to an erosion of their privileges and preferences. For people of this view it is better to put up with the imperfections of the status quo than to endorse an arrangement that might be objectively better but could lead to something perceived as far worse. A good many people who are less political fear any change in political arrangements that might lead to reduced British subsidies to the North, which for all its troubles enjoys higher level of social services than the South does (pensions, child benefits, welfare, and so on).

What makes it especially difficult to build a dominant coalition between moderate elements of the two communities—a coalition that could endorse something along the lines of the arrangements agreed to at Sunningdale and Hillsborough—is the divided leadership on both sides. Among Catholics, moderates represented by the SDLP are intimidated by the Provisional IRA and increasingly outflanked by the Sinn Fein. The result is that traditional moderates, forced to compete with more radical voices or face irrelevance, are less moderate than they once were, at the same time as they represent a smaller share of their own community. A similar polarization is occurring among Protestants. The more moderate voices (such as the centrist Alliance party, which also includes Catholics), and what might be described as the less radical Official Unionist party, are circumscribed in their appeal by the Democratic Unionist party. The net result of these political dynamics on both sides is that compromise is difficult to arrange, much less sustain.

That paramilitary forces exist on both sides further complicates the political picture. Beyond questions of formulas and negotiating processes is the reality that any political progress is vulnerable to interruption, either by a direct assault on those involved or by actions that create a climate in which dialogue and compromise become all but impossible. Last, there is no consensus among those outsiders with influence in Northern Ireland. Successive British governments have been unhappy with the responsibility but uncertain how to discharge it. Within Ireland there are differences between the parties, with one, Fianna Fail, closer to the nationalist position than is the principal alternative, Fine Gael. And in the United States there remain substantial sympathy and support for the nationalist position, support that at times manifests itself in the form of contributions to the Provisional IRA.

It is thus difficult to find fault with this sober assessment of the predicament of Northern Ireland:

> There are no simple "solutions" to the Northern Ireland problem, neither in the political context nor in terms of security policy . . . It should also be emphasized that there are no quick solutions. Many of the political and social problems which fuel the Northern Ireland conflict are very deep-rooted indeed. It would be foolish to assume that either loyalists or nationalists can suddenly jettison several centuries of real and perceived injustice, oppression and struggle. Such cultural baggage cannot neatly be packed away in some convenient political left-luggage office. Progress and reconciliation in Northern Ireland can only be achieved at a painfully gradual pace.[5]

## An Approach to Policy: Building Trust?

But if no solution exists and the status quo is costly and promises no end, what then? The answer is suggested by the final sentence of the quotation above: progress and reconciliation can be achieved only slowly, if at all. This sobering assessment is supported by the considerable opposition that emerged to destroy the modest agreement reached at Sunningdale and that is threatening to undermine the Anglo-Irish Accord of 1985. Recent political developments in the North (where loyalists are busy protesting against Hillsborough) and South (where there is considerable disillusionment with the accord's actual impact) suggest that even such modest steps in the direction of condominium and devolution are more than the political environment can now support.

If this pessimistic assessment proves incorrect (and, even more important, if it does not), an important component of policy must consist of confidence-building measures designed to lessen the ignorance and mistrust that characterizes relations between Northern Ireland's two communities. Such measures are justified on two grounds: they can ease tension in the absence of grand political arrangements that solve the problem in its entirety or in large part, and they can create the sort of understanding that might eventually make it slightly less difficult to bring about positive results associated with traditional diplomacy. Such confidence-building measures can take many forms. Given Northern Ireland's high rate of unemployment (20 percent or more) and its low rate of economic growth, investment that led to improved economic conditions would lighten the atmosphere of despair. Investment projects that linked Ulster and the Irish Republic are one possibility. Even more valuable might be undertakings that brought together the two communities in the workplace. This sort of gesture would not only help relieve poverty but would accomplish the additional function of reducing some of what divides the two communities. So too would educational and cultural undertakings that brought together Catholic and Protestant. A prime example of what is needed is the range of economic activities sponsored by the International Fund for Ireland (IFI), an international organization established in 1986 by the British and Irish governments "to promote economic and social advance and to encourage contact, dialogue and reconciliation between nationalists and unionists throughout Ireland."[6]

Other steps would also help. Judicial reform is one possibility; courts with only one judge and no jury are bound to be controversial. Even more important might be measures to reduce the segregation between Catholics and Protestants in the North. School segregation is especially harmful, as new generations of Catholics grow up reading different (and often one-sided) textbooks, and never have informal contacts with Protestants in classrooms and playing fields.

Even such modest measures will not be easy to introduce. Confidence building is not a panacea. On each side of the conflict are paramilitary forces that oppose normalization and bridge building because they would reduce the chances for radical change of the sort that the forces profess to want. This underlines the need for security: political progress in Northern Ireland cannot be understood as something apart from security and stability. All are necessarily part of an integrated whole, for no moderates can long survive in an environment where radical elements can intimidate or, worse yet, prevent the moderates from entering into a dialogue and making compromise political arrangements.[7]

Security arrangements in Northern Ireland can also build confidence. The principal police force in the North, the Royal Ulster Constabulary (RUC), is one of the few institutions in which Catholics and Protestants serve together. And to the extent that the RUC (which is still predominantly Protestant) is perceived as dispatching law and order fairly (a perception that is increasing), it will be accepted by the Catholics as evidence that the majority is not necessarily devoted to making life miserable for the minority. The behavior of the virtually all-Protestant Ulster Defense Regiment (an army force recruited in the province to back up the British Army) can make the same point by its behavior.

What would not build confidence would be a British military withdrawal. The British presence, although at times exacerbating tensions in the province, is mostly a reflection of the troubles rather than a cause of them. Were many or all troops withdrawn, there would likely be a marked increase in violence. Even worse, such a move could trigger a unilateral declaration of independence by the unionists, which would in turn bring about a major political crisis affecting everyone with a stake in the province.

This last caution serves as a useful reminder. Frustration with the status quo in Northern Ireland ought not to drive those with responsibility for the province into taking steps that could make a bad situation worse. The key external actor in Northern Ireland —the British government—is in the unenviable position of having sufficient influence to make things worse but not enough to make them significantly better. Diplomatic activism, particularly if it includes a large Irish dimension, is likely only to feed loyalist resistance and nationalist fantasies. If such a dimension is required even to making power sharing viable for local Catholics, then it will be best if there is no formal initiative from the top down (from London to the province). The only realistic and constructive course for this most intractable of conflicts may be efforts from the bottom up that use a mix of confidence-building measures—political, economic, and security-related—to reduce resentments and the sense of being besieged.

# 7

## RIPENESS AND ITS

## IMPLICATIONS FOR

## POLICY

---

Conflict is the rule in international affairs. This is as true today as it has been for centuries. The task before diplomats and would-be statesmen is to search for ways of eliminating conflict. Failing this, their task is to regulate adversarial relationships so that they do not erupt in war or, if they do, that the violence is of limited duration and intensity.

Ripeness will often determine the success of these diplomatic efforts. Whether negotiation will succeed or fail will hinge on the shared perception by the disputants that an accord is desirable, the existence of leadership on all sides that is either sufficiently strong to sustain a compromise or so weak that a compromise cannot be avoided, a formula involving some benefits for all participants, and a commonly accepted diplomatic process. In the preceding chapters I have argued that ripeness accounted for several negotiating successes. The talks at Lancaster House that led to the establishment of Zimbabwe, the Beagle Channel dispute between Chile and Argentina, Camp David, Afghanistan, the Iran-Iraq War, possibly Namibia and Angola—all demonstrate that under the right circumstances diplomacy can help resolve conflicts and negotiations can succeed.

At least as often, the absence of ripeness explains why diplomats fail. Here the list is long: the Middle East beyond Camp David, Cyprus, the Aegean, India and Pakistan, Lebanon, the Falklands, Central America, Northern Ireland, South Africa. One could add to this list many of the examples of successes, in that for years many of them resisted the best efforts of diplomats to resolve them. The lesson to be learned from these situations is not that diplomats could have succeeded had they done things differently, but that success is sometimes beyond reach because those at the core of disputes are unwilling or unable to make peace.

Ripeness is anything but a natural condition; in most conflicts the main ingredients of success are absent. Rarely are these missing ingredients either negotiating formulas or inadequate negotiating techniques, the two matters with which observers and even experienced diplomats most often concern themselves. What tends to be absent instead is a far rarer commodity: leaders who find settlement preferable to conflict, and who either are strong enough to convince people in and out of the government of this or so weak that they cannot resist the pressures exerted by others. In the absence of such leadership, the temptation is for mediators or others with a stake in promoting peace to compensate with heightened diplomatic activity for what is missing. But too much diplomacy or mediation in an unripe situation can be counterproductive. Such activism, no matter how well intentioned or politically useful as a demonstration of concern, can lead parties in a dispute to avoid facing reality and taking tough but necessary decisions. Paradoxically, outside activism can actually discourage the emergence of a situation in which outside activism might be highly productive. Diplomatic activism can also trigger preemptive steps by one of the disputants (to frustrate or prevent negotiation), or, if the diplomacy is unsuccessful, it can stimulate unilateral steps that may be provocative.

Some will argue that this wariness of diplomatic activism is unwarranted, and that there is little to be lost and possibly much to be gained from trying to solve dangerous and costly disputes. This is simply not so. Diplomatic initiatives launched in unripe circumstances are almost certain to fail. When they do they can discredit otherwise good proposals, diminishing their appeal and utility should circumstances change. In addition, premature diplomacy can weaken the credibility of high-level diplomats and waste their limited time. Last, acting against the odds can create an atmosphere of despair in which local political leaders most opposed to compromise are likely to thrive. Good intentions, or the need to satisfy widespread political pressures to act, is not enough with so much at stake.

There is much evidence that diplomatic activism often has a high cost. Henry Kissinger opposed a Middle East initiative by the United States in 1969 and 1970 at least in part because its likely failure could have led to war.[1] In the Falklands, American activism may have contributed to the delusion of the Argentine government that its behavior would not lead to a disastrous war, or if it did lead to war that the United States would pressure Great Britain to capitulate. Too much activism on Cyprus only raises Turkish suspicions and induces Greek Cypriots to avoid tough decisions, in the belief that the United States will pressure Turkey to deliver the Turkish Cypriots. In South Africa, Western sanctions appear to have reduced the Afrikaners' propensity to compromise, without strengthening the position of blacks who do want to compromise. And in the Middle East, too much outside pressure for diplomatic progress reinforces Israel's stubbornness while strengthening the illusion in the Arab world that the key to peace lies in a willingness by the United States to pressure Israel, rather than in a willingness to compromise on the part of the Arabs. Secretary of State George Shultz may well have accomplished more in the Middle East by staying at home in the latter months of 1988 than he had in all four of his shuttles earlier in the year.

This is not an argument for doing nothing. A hands-off posture can be politically unrealistic and unsustainable. There is often much pressure for a great power to act, both from within and from without. Standing back may also be irresponsible. And to allow a catastrophe to happen in the mistaken view that crisis and tragedy are prerequisites to successful diplomacy not only ignores the costs of conflict but is shortsighted: some costly conflicts have not led to settlement, and some settlements have not been preceded by costly conflicts. But doing something does not necessarily mean negotiating. Often it means undertaking a range of activities—political, economic, and even military, private and public—to change attitudes and calculations. This can make negotiations prosper in the future and lessen the chances that conflict will break out in the interim.

This last point raises the important question of whether crises constitute an additional prerequisite for diplomatic progress. In some instances crises or wars clearly precede progress. The Middle East war of 1973 set the stage for Camp David, by strengthening the position of Anwar Sadat and reminding the Israelis that they could neither ignore diplomacy nor assume that they could always deter or dominate a three-front war. Similarly, the confrontation of April 1987 in the Aegean stimulated a quiet dialogue between Greece and Turkey that culminated in January 1988 in a meeting at Davos, Switzerland, between Prime Minister Papandreou of Greece and Prime Minister Ozal of Turkey, at which the two agreed to establish a more regular dialogue and a direct telephone link.

Yet few crises or wars bring about progress in negotiation. Although the Middle East war of 1973 led to Camp David, those of 1948 and 1967 (both one-sided Israeli victories) led to diplomatic stalemate. The wars of 1971 in South Asia and of 1974 on Cyprus have similarly failed to promote diplomatic accomplishment. Neither the crisis that preceded the conflict of the Falklands/Malvinas in 1982 nor the war itself contributed to successful negotiation. A number of crises in South Africa, from those of Sharpeville and Soweto to the violent clashes of 1986, have done little to generate compromise. And in Northern Ireland there is no shortage of incidents and crises, but little evidence that any have furthered political progress.

As a rule, crisis or near-crisis can contribute to diplomacy if there is a shared recognition that steps must be taken to avoid developments that will be costly to all concerned. A crisis will promote negotiation only if it leaves the parties believing that accord is in their interest, and either strong enough to compromise or so weak that they have to compromise. The conflict in Cyprus of 1974 and the war in the Falklands left the victor with little incentive to parley. The confrontation in the Aegean in March 1987 appears to have had a more benign effect, but not significantly so. It is too soon to conclude whether the Palestinian uprising will serve the interests of reconciliation. Although it is possible that it will have given the Palestinians the confidence to compromise and Israelis the incentive to, it is just as possible that the rebellion has hardened Israeli attitudes and that only its ultimate lack of effect persuaded the PLO's leaders that compromise on their part was unavoidable.

Negotiations prosper most when no major diversion occurs. Camp David could well have failed had a terrorist attack been mounted successfully in Israel at the time. Current efforts in the Middle East and Northern Ireland are similarly at risk; future efforts in South Africa may well be. Governments should be aware that behavior in seemingly unrelated spheres can affect the course of negotiations. This may require steps to decrease the vulnerability of the parties and the negotiations to disruption, or steps to discount the impact of disruption if it occurs. These can range from the physical (reducing vulnerability to terrorism) to the political (warning the public of possible attempts to disrupt, so that the sense of shock and crisis will be diluted if they are made). And one must not overlook the importance of luck, for events can so alter calculations that what seemed ripe for agreement becomes suddenly unripe.

The passage of time has an uneven effect, though its effect seems greatest where conflict is intense: in the Iran-Iraq War, Afghanistan, and Zimbabwe, for example, the passage of time seems to have increased the pressures on leaders to compromise. This effect is not constant: for a while time works in the opposite way, as the leaders' investment in a dispute at first makes it more difficult for them to compromise their objectives. But at some point exhaustion can be a powerful inducement to parley. In conflicts of low intensity, time appears to have just the opposite effect. The cost of perpetuating the status quo seems less than the potential risks of compromise. People and societies adjust. Cyprus, Northern Ireland, the Middle East, Central America, even Lebanon—in none of these cases is the conflict so painful that the parties prefer compromise to staying the course, no matter how bleak this persistence may appear to outsiders.

Guerrilla and civil wars can be especially difficult to bring to an end. They are relatively easy for the guerrilla side to sustain, requiring little more than small amounts of weapons (often captured) and personnel. That such struggles tend to be strongly ideological also works against "reasonable" compromise, negotiation, and tradeoffs. Making things even more complicated is that guerrilla leadership is often divided. And perhaps most important, guerrilla leaders are unlike the leaders of nation-states, who are accountable for a broad range of services and policies, for guerrillas normally have the luxury of being able to focus on one enterprise. This too makes conflict easier to sustain.

Resolving conflict often requires caution and modesty. There are limits to the ability of outsiders to reshape perceptions or otherwise "deliver" recalcitrant participants. In the Middle East, southern Africa, Northern Ireland, and the eastern Mediterranean, local parties have shown repeatedly their ability to frustrate the will of outsiders who come forward with plans for solving the region's ills. Too much outside pressure is perceived as bullying, and this is likely to strengthen the position of rejectionist leaders who can claim to be protecting the nation against outside interference. And pressure is in any event difficult to manufacture: there is rarely domestic or international consensus for pressure in a certain direction; sanctions are terribly difficult to orchestrate, and in most instances patrons who impose sanctions can be replaced by other patrons.

Except in those atypical instances where the participant depends almost totally on the mediator's goodwill, outsiders must also contend with how rare it is for leverage to work only in one direction. The United States, for example, must balance its interest in promoting regional negotiation with other interests, ranging from maintaining access to raw materials or military bases to preventing the expansion of Soviet influence or the proliferation of nuclear weapons. The same is true for the Soviet Union or even the United Nations, which suffers the additional handicap of being only as strong as the five permanent members of the Security Council want it to be (the United States, the Soviet Union, China, Great Britain, and France).

External influence can however be critical, particularly if a disputant is highly dependent on external support, and if the domestic politics of the patron allow the support to be terminated. Soviet and South African influence seem to have been critical in bringing about a settlement of the Angolan conflict. By contrast, there is little evidence that outsiders are able or in some instances even willing to play such a role in the dispute between Greece and Turkey, or in those in Northern Ireland, South Africa, South Asia, Central America, and the Middle East.

Ripeness is not either totally present or totally absent. Often only parts of a problem are ripe for negotiation; it would be an error in most cases not to address part of a problem in an attempt to solve the entire problem. There is some risk in this—the easier unsolved parts of the problem can in principle lubricate the more difficult ones—but this danger tends to be outweighed by the need to reduce tensions and in the process demonstrate that progress is possible.

Camp David provides a lesson. Egypt had no mandate to negotiate on behalf of the Palestinians, and Prime Minister Begin's government had little desire to satisfy Palestinian concerns. The Camp David accords would never have come about had the United States sought to make a separate settlement between Cairo and Jerusalem contingent on a solution to the larger Middle East problem. The breakthrough in Angola and Namibia might well have proved beyond reach had diplomats sought to define the exact shape of Angola's future political arrangements. Current efforts in the Middle East are likely to progress only if some of the

Confidence building is also an important alternative to doing nothing and traditional negotiation. In regional disputes confidence building can not only decrease the chance of conflict by miscalculation, but also contribute to stability over the longer term by fostering change at the personal level, rather than just the governmental level. Often this sort of person-to-person diplomacy, which brings together citizens of rival states or entities when the officials cannot be brought together, is characterized as "track two" diplomacy. Informal conversations and meetings on this second track supplement what takes place on the more traditional, formal first track. Track two diplomacy can have a modest impact over time, if not quite the impact that its advocates suggest.[3] And confidence building can satisfy at least in part the political pressures for some sign of effort to defuse a crisis or solve a long-standing dispute.

In Cyprus, for example, in addition to supporting the United Nations peacekeeping force, the withdrawal of Turkish troops, and a relaxation of the Greek Cypriot economic embargo that constrains the North, the United States should promote enterprises that benefit both communities and require their participation and support, especially educational and business enterprises. Such an approach might make an outbreak of fighting less likely and blur the island's lines of partition, so that the next generation of political leaders might be willing to explore opportunities for diplomacy that this generation so far has not.

In the Middle East, in addition to promoting confidence building of the kind just mentioned, the United States should encourage confidence building of another sort. Specifically, representatives of Israel and the Palestinians could create an environment more conducive to negotiations by articulating not what futures they are seeking, but what futures they are not seeking. It would be useful for the Palestinians to complement their statements accepting Israel as a permanent state in the region with a repudiation of the so-called phased solution, according to which the formation of a separate Palestinian state would be the first step in a process leading to control over all the land west of the Jordan

most contentious issues are postponed or left ambiguous. Indeed, issues of final status and internal political arrangements often are best postponed if the intention is to bring about an agreement that at least resolves some elements of a dispute and sets the stage for further progress down the road.

Modesty is important in another sense as well. In many conflicts that are in essence intractable, efforts to settle them once and for all will by definition fail. Diplomats would do well to put aside objectives of perfect solution in which questions of sovereignty and territory are decided and look instead at halfway measures (autonomy and condominium arrangements, for example). These will be better than the status quo, and can build confidence and the prospects for something more ambitious and permanent. Northern Ireland comes to mind here; so does the Middle East. If formulas become too fixed and far-reaching, they can actually impede diplomatic progress.

Last, it is important to keep in mind that ripeness is dynamic; it can emerge as easily as it can disappear. What may have been a ripe moment in Lebanon in 1982 soon passed. Time allowed the defeated parties to recover and increase their political requirements beyond a point where they could be accepted by Israel, once victorious but increasingly discouraged. Similarly, it is doubtful that what was accomplished at Camp David would have been possible months later, had the meeting failed and participants been forced to defend their possible compromises without having those of the other side to point to.

In short, ripeness is an important concept that deserves wider currency. It lends itself to negotiations of all sorts. It is of value to analysts and also to practitioners. Where conflicts are intractable, assessments of ripeness can allow diplomats to avoid doing things that are useless or counterproductive. The absence of ripeness can alert diplomats to the need to promote confidence building. And just as important, ripeness can help practitioners who have limited time, energy, and focus to choose where to concentrate their resources. If agendas are to be realized, they must reflect reality as well as resolve.

## Policy in the Absence of Ripeness

If traditional diplomatic activism is often not the answer and if crises and wars are to be avoided, nations must still decide what to do: "If 'not ripe' is the diagnosis . . . getting people in a room together and employing all sorts of careful procedural means to foster negotiation will likely be to no avail. The basic condition for a negotiated agreement will not be met since possible agreements appear inferior to at least one side in comparison with its unilateral alternatives. When this is the case, strategy should focus *not* on the negotiation process but instead on actions *away* from the table that can reshape perceptions in a manner that generates a zone of possible agreement" (italics in original).[2]

There are constructive things to be done away from the table. One alternative to traditional diplomatic activism is private and public education. A would-be mediator can try to get governments and their constituents to recognize the costs of disagreement and the potential benefits of agreement, as well as to expect compromises. Public diplomacy can also prepare leaders and the public for the costs of the negotiating process itself (increased terrorism, for instance), thereby reducing the likelihood that diplomacy will be undermined by unfolding events. Educational diplomacy can create an environment in which leaders will be permitted or even pressured to reach a deal. That public discourse, if carefully controlled, can be useful in the phase leading to negotiations is too often obscured by the traditional bias of diplomats in favor of secrecy (admittedly necessary in many cases once negotiations are under way).

In the Middle East, for example, the United States could point out to Arabs and Israelis in and out of government the costs and risks inherent in the status quo. It could also make clear what steps or outcomes it views as counterproductive, and outline elements of what it considers constructive gestures as well as a fair and stable settlement. And it could announce what it is prepared to do to facilitate negotiation and reward compromise. Much the

same could be done for South Africa, Cyprus, or Sou[...] would not be interference in the specific political c[...] other state (which is always likely to backfire) but r[...] pation in its debate. There is some unavoidable risk [...] but this must be weighed against the costs of tradi[...] matic activism on the one hand and inaction on [...] none of the cases presented in the preceding chap[...] necessary or advisable to begin formal negotiations; [...] come about only when the parties made clear th[...] prepared to negotiate in good faith and that there was [...] chance of progress.

Mediators and other interested parties can also w[...] rectly to create conditions of ripeness. Military assi[...] ligence support, security guarantees, the commit[...] alliance—all these can be extended (or held back[...] leaders to take risks for peace. Similarly, leaders can [...] ened by gestures and steps ranging from high-level [...] nomic commitments and projects.

Here too one can cite examples from the past, as [...] dates for the future. Covert aid to various resistanc[...] can create conditions in which governments will [...] compromise is preferable to endless conflict. Afg[...] Angola come to mind; so does Cambodia, where A[...] nese, and Thai support for various resistance for[...] have contributed to Vietnam's declared decisio[...] decadelong occupation of Cambodia by 1990. The [...] Nicaragua is stark, for there it is in part the curtailn[...] ican aid that diminished the government's propensi[...] mise. Similarly, aid to Israel can in principle convi[...] that they have no alternative to negotiating in goo[...] at the same time reassuring Israel that negotiating [...] poses no unacceptable risk. It is quite possible too[...] political and military support for Iraq (together wit[...] and military isolation of Iran) helped convince Ira[...] uing the war was futile. Many of these same pol[...] applied to other regional conflicts.

River. Similarly, Israel could contribute to diplomatic prospects by ruling out both perpetuation of the status quo and annexation of the occupied territories. In both instances, actions could be found that would give additional significance to these statements (the PLO could make good on its rejection of terrorism and remove the anti-Zionist clauses in its charter, and Israel could allow greater self-rule on the West Bank and Gaza and reduce its military presence).

In the Aegean, confidence building of a more traditional kind should be introduced. The agreement in January 1988 to create a dedicated communications link between leaders of the two governments may help to avoid escalation should an incident occur. Greece and Turkey could adapt for their use the Soviet-American agreement on incidents at sea and establish an Aegean regime of nonharassment and rules of the road. They might also agree to exchange advance notice of the timing, location, and size of military exercises. Such steps would not address the core Aegean issues, but they would make an accident less likely and build trust.

In South Africa confidence building in the economic, educational, and cultural realms could be used to break down some of the barriers between the white and black populations. One can also imagine how confidence building might contribute to a similar reduction in tensions between Catholics and Protestants in Northern Ireland. And although confidence building of this sort would be helpful in reducing mistrust between Indians and Pakistanis, South Asia also warrants a more specific regime of confidence-building measures designed to make the development and use of nuclear weapons less likely, ranging from advance notice of missile flight tests and agreements not to attack nuclear installations, to possible no-first-use pacts and intelligence-sharing arrangements.

Confidence building need not result only from formal agreements; it can be informal when politics require it. Circumstances in which compromise and deescalation would be even more difficult to bring about can be prevented by tacit regimes of reciprocal restraint—for example, by wartime understandings that certain categories of targets are off limits, or that chemical or nuclear weapons are off limits, or by avoiding provocative statements and actions during peacetime.

Nor must confidence building be mutual. Unilateral gestures or steps that could set the stage for more ambitious diplomacy ought not to be held hostage to mutual undertakings, informal or formal. Decisions to reduce or otherwise restructure military forces can be taken outside formal arms control venues if they contribute to stability. Israel may want to relax administrative controls in the occupied territories to reduce pressures, even absent a reciprocal gesture by the Palestinians. Turkey may choose to withdraw some of its forces from Cyprus to create an atmosphere in which Greek Cypriot politicians would find it easier to engage their Turkish Cypriot counterparts. A focus on negotiation should not blind states to what they can do unilaterally to reduce tensions and promote stability.

Indeed, a focus on negotiations should not blind the United States to other policy paths. Of course negotiated solutions to regional conflicts would be desirable, but in many situations the parties are not ready or able to make the necessary compromises. When they are not—when the dispute is not ripe for resolution—it is almost always counterproductive for the United States to proceed with negotiations as if they were. Fortunately there are alternatives. The United States can say and do things to reduce the likelihood of violence, while possibly creating circumstances in which negotiations might prove both appropriate and successful. This is a conclusion that should only disappoint those unwilling to accept history's message: that in a world of men and nation-states conflict can only be managed, not eliminated.

# NOTES

## INTRODUCTION

1. Robert A. Isaak, *American Diplomacy and World Power* (New York: St. Martin's, 1977), 21.

2. See Thomas Sowell, *A Conflict of Visions: Ideological Origins of Political Struggles* (New York: William Morrow, 1987).

3. Joseph A. Califano, Jr., "The Health-Care Chaos," *New York Times Magazine*, March 20, 1988, p. 56.

## I. THINKING ABOUT NEGOTIATIONS

1. See I. William Zartman, *Ripe for Resolution: Conflict and Intervention in Africa* (New York: Oxford University Press, 1985), chapters 1, 6; Zartman, "Ripening Conflict, Ripe Moment, Formula, and Mediation," in *Perspectives on Negotiation*, ed. Diane B. Bendahmane and John W. McDonald (Washington: Center for the Study of Foreign Affairs, Foreign Service Institute, U.S. Department of State, 1986), 205–227; and Zartman, "The Strategy of Preventive Diplomacy in Third World Conflicts," in *Managing U.S.-Soviet Rivalry: Problems of Crisis Prevention*, ed. Alexander L. George (Boulder: Westview, 1983), 341–363. See also Louis Kriesberg, "'Ripeness' and the Initiation of De-escalation Moves" (paper presented to the International Studies Association, April 1987, published in *Negotiation Journal*, October 1987).

2. Fred Charles Iklé's influential *How Nations Negotiate* (New York: Praeger, 1964) is an early example of this approach. Two excellent and more recent works are Howard Raiffa, *The Art and Science of Negotiation* (Cambridge: Harvard University Press, 1982) and David A. Lax and James K. Sebenius, *The Manager as Negotiator: Bargaining for Cooperation and Competitive Gain* (New York: Free Press, 1986).

3. For a popular example of this genre see Roger Fisher and William Ury, *Getting to Yes* (Boston: Houghton Mifflin, 1981).

4. Hans Binnendijk, ed., *National Negotiating Styles* (Washington: Center for the Study of Foreign Affairs, Foreign Service Institute, U.S. Department of State, 1987) contains interesting assessments of Chinese, Soviet, Japanese, French, Egyptian, and Mexican approaches to negotiation.

5. There were of course other factors as well, including the mutual entrapment of armies. For a valuable assessment of these accords and Kissinger's diplomacy see Jeffrey Z. Rubin, ed., *Dynamics of Third Party Intervention: Kissinger in the Middle East* (New York: Praeger, 1981).

6. William B. Quandt, *Camp David: Peacemaking and Politics* (Washington: Brookings Institution, 1986), 321, 331.

7. Background to the Beagle Channel dispute is provided by "Beagle Channel Negotiations," parts A and B (Cambridge: John F. Kennedy School of Government Case Program, Cases C15-88-796–7, 1988).

8. Some details can be found in the *New York Times*, November 30, 1984, sec. A, p. 5.

9. The phrase is from Jeffrey Davidow. For a valuable account and analysis of the Rhodesia talks see his book *A Peace in Southern Africa: The Lancaster House Conference on Rhodesia, 1979* (Boulder: Westview, 1984). In this discussion I make liberal use of Davidow's monograph, as well as of chapter 4, "Negotiating Zimbabwe's Independence," in Bendahmane and McDonald, *Perspectives on Negotiation*.

10. The text of the Afghan accords is in the *New York Times*, April 15, 1988, sec. A, p. 12.

11. The text of the agreement is in the *New York Times*, July 21, 1988, sec. A, p. 7.

12. There were in fact two agreements signed: a three-way agreement by South Africa, Cuba, and Angola on arrangements governing independence for Namibia, and a separate pact between Cuba and Angola on the withdrawal from Namibia of Cuban forces. For the text of the accords of December 22 and background to them see Paul Lewis, "Angola and Namibia Accords Signed," *New York Times*, December 23, 1988, sec. A, p. 6.

13. For an excellent analysis of why agreement proved possible see David B. Ottoway, "The Peace Process in Southern Africa," *Washington Post*, December 23, 1988, sec. A, p. 14. A separate accord calling for a cease-fire and beginning the process of internal political reconciliation was not reached until June 22, 1989.

14. For useful background and analysis see Efraim Karsh, *The Iran-Iraq War: A Military Analysis* (London: International Institute for Strategic Studies, 1987).

15. The text of Resolution 598 is in the *New York Times*, July 19, 1988, sec. A, p. 8. Besides calling for an immediate cease-fire and withdrawal to international boundaries, the resolution states that the United Nations will "explore . . . the question of entrusting an impartial body with inquiring into responsibility for the conflict." This falls far short of what Iran desired, which was nothing less than to have Iraq blamed and to receive reparations.

16. Long excerpts from Khomeini's statement are in the *New York Times*, July 23, 1988, p. 5.

17. For background see "Falklands/Malvinas (A): Breakdown of Negotiations," (Cambridge: John F. Kennedy School of Government, case C95-86-661, 1986); and "Mediation Attempts in the Falkland/Malvinas Crisis," in Bendahmane and McDonald, *Perspectives on Negotiation*, chapter 2, especially 51–72.

18. For background to this phase of the crisis see "Falklands/Malvinas B: The Haig Mediation Effort," (Cambridge: John F. Kennedy School of Government, case C16-86-662, 1987); and Bendahmane and McDonald, *Perspectives on Negotiation*, 72–90. For Haig's account see his memoirs, *Caveat: Realism, Reagan and Foreign Policy* (New York: Macmillan, 1984), 261–302.

19. My discussion of Lebanon draws on "The Reagan Administration and Lebanon" (Cambridge: John F. Kennedy School of Government, case C15-88-803, 1988); Itamar Rabinovich, *The War for Lebanon, 1970–1985* (Ithaca: Cornell University Press, 1985); and Haig, *Caveat*, 317–352. Haig places too much emphasis on the administration's disarray and not enough on flawed strategy and Lebanon's problems; nevertheless, his is one of the few insider's accounts available.

20. One readable and useful introduction to Lebanon is Milton Viorst, "A Reporter at Large: The Christian Enclave," *New Yorker*, October 3, 1988, pp. 40–71.

## 2. THE MIDDLE EAST

1. For representative expressions of this perspective see Jimmy Carter, "Middle East Peace: New Opportunities," *Washington Quarterly* 10, no. 3 (Summer 1987): 5–14; Harold H. Saunders, "Arabs and Israelis: A Political Strategy," *Foreign Affairs* (Winter 1985–86): 304–325; and Robert G. Neumann, Shireen T. Hunter, and Frederick W. Axelgard, *Revitalizing U.S. Leadership in the Middle East* (Washington: Center for Strategic and International Studies, 1988).

2. Not surprisingly, there is an enormous literature on the Arab-Israeli dispute, and in particular on the causes and consequences of the 1967 war. For a range of perspectives on the dispute in general see David Shipler, *Arab and Jew: Wounded Spirits in a Promised Land* (New York:

Times Books, 1986); Maxine Rodinson, *Israel and the Arabs* (London: Penguin, 1970); Alvin Rubinstein, ed., *The Arab-Israeli Conflict: Perspectives* (New York: Praeger, 1984); and Joan Peters, *From Time Immemorial: The Origins of the Arab-Jewish Conflict over Palestine* (New York: Harper and Row, 1984). For an interesting analysis of American policy see Steven L. Spiegel, *The Other Arab-Israeli Conflict: Making America's Middle East Policy, from Truman to Reagan* (Chicago: University of Chicago Press, 1985). On the 1967 war a useful work is Walter Laqueur, *The Road to War: The Origins and Aftermath of the Arab-Israeli Conflict, 1967–8* (London: Penguin, 1970). For an assessment of the years following the 1967 war see William B. Quandt, *Decade of Decisions: American Policy toward the Arab-Israeli Conflict, 1967–1976* (Berkeley: University of California Press, 1977).

3. Useful assessments of this period are William B. Quandt, ed., *The Middle East: Ten Years after Camp David* (Washington: Brookings Institution, 1988); and Aaron David Miller, "The Arab-Israeli Conflict, 1967–1987: A Retrospective," *Middle East Journal* 41, no. 3 (Summer 1987): 349–360.

4. The best case study of the Camp David accords is William B. Quandt, *Camp David: Peacemaking and Politics* (Washington: Brookings Institution, 1986).

5. The text of the accord of February 11, 1985, between Hussein and Arafat is reprinted in Yehoshafat Harkabi, *Israel's Fateful Hour* (New York: Harper and Row, 1988), 241–242.

6. A text of United Nations Security Council Resolution 242 of November 22, 1967, is in John Norton Moore, ed., *The Arab-Israeli Dispute: Readings and Documents* (Princeton: Princeton University Press, 1977), 1084.

7. Much of my analysis and of my later discussion of the uprising's effects are drawn from *The Impact of the Uprising: Report of a Fact-Finding Mission for the Washington Institute's Presidential Study Group on U.S. Policy in the Middle East* (Washington: Washington Institute for Near East Policy, 1988). The six-member mission, in which I took part, visited Israel, Jordan, Egypt, and the West Bank for ten days in March 1988.

8. For a clear articulation of American policy at the time see Richard W. Murphy, "An American Vision of Peace in the Middle East" (address to the Washington Institute on Near East Policy, Washington, April 18, 1988, published by the State Department's Bureau of Public Affairs as no. 1067 in its Current Policy series). For background documents that spell out the proposal in detail see "U.S. Policy in the Middle East," published by the State Department's Bureau of Public Affairs as Document no. 27, June 1988.

9. Excerpts from Hussein's address of July 31, 1988, are printed in the *New York Times*, August 1, 1988, sec. A, p. 4. For an interesting assessment of Hussein's motives see Karen Elliott House, "By Abandoning Palestinians to the PLO, Hussein Hopes to Protect Country, Crown," *Wall Street Journal*, August 2, 1988, p. 17.

10. An excerpt of the statement, distributed in early June 1988 at the Arab summit in Algiers under the name of Bassam Abu Sharif, Yasir Arafat's press spokesman, appears in the *New York Times*, June 22, 1988, sec. A, p. 27.

11. Resolution 338 (October 22, 1973) called for a cease-fire and for the implementation of Security Council Resolution 242 of 1967. For background to the agreements of 1975 between the United States and Israel see Spiegel, *The Other Arab-Israeli Conflict*, 300–302.

12. The text of the joint statement issued by Yasir Arafat and the delegation of American Jews is in the *New York Times*, December 8, 1988, sec. A, p. 10.

13. For a summary of these hectic few weeks of diplomacy see Don Oberdorfer, "U.S.-PLO Relationship a Diplomatic Roller Coaster," *Washington Post*, December 18, 1988, pp. 1, 30.

14. For some healthy skepticism see "The Arafat Shuttle," *New Republic*, January 9–16, 1989, pp. 9–12.

15. See Meron Benvenisti, *The West Bank Data Project: A Survey of Israel's Policies* (Washington: American Enterprise Institute, 1984), 64. See also Conor Cruise O'Brien's important article "Why Israel Can't Take 'Bold Steps' for Peace," *Atlantic*, October 1985, pp. 45–55. For a more detailed (but equally pessimistic) survey of possible outcomes see *The West Bank and Gaza: Israel's Options for Peace* (Tel Aviv: Jaffa Center for Strategic Studies, 1989).

16. For the origins of this notion see Susan Lee Hattis, *The Bi-national Idea in Palestine during Mandatory Times* (Haifa: Shikmona, 1970).

17. As regards this last idea see Dan Kurzman, "Models for the Middle East: Benelux and Danzig," *New York Times*, December 10, 1988, p. 27. There is a good deal of literature on the feasibility of a Palestinian state, including discussions of arrangements that might make it less objectionable to Israel. See Avi Plascov, *A Palestinian State? Examining the Alternatives* (London: International Institute for Strategic Studies, 1981); Avraham Wachman, "A Peace Plan," *New Republic*, September 5, 1988, pp. 20–22; Mark A. Heller, *A Palestinian State: The Implications for Israel* (Cambridge: Harvard University Press, 1983); and Jerome M. Segal, *Creating the Palestinian State: A Strategy for Peace* (Chicago: Lawrence Hill, 1989). For a negative view see Daniel Pipes, "A Nightmare for the Arabs and for Israel," *New York Times*, April 25, 1988, sec. A, p. 21.

18. See for example American Friends Service Committee, *A Compassionate Peace: A Future for the Middle East* (New York: Hill and Wang, 1982).

19. For an impassioned yet reasoned view along these lines see Yehoshafat Harkabi, *Israel's Fateful Hour* (New York: Harper and Row, 1988).

20. One idea is to place Gaza under the supervision of the United Nations, much as the Baltic city of Danzig was placed under the aegis of the League of Nations. See Gene R. La Rocque, "Models for the Middle East: Benelux and Danzig," *New York Times*, December 10, 1988, p. 27.

21. Texts of both the Camp David accords and the Reagan Plan, as well as a good many other key documents, can be found in Walter Laqueur and Barry Rubin, eds., *The Israel-Arab Reader: A Documentary History of the Middle East Conflict* (London: Pelican, 1984).

22. For an assessment that concludes that the Jordanian option is no longer viable see Mordechai Nisan, "The 'Jordanian Option': Is It Politically Feasible?" *Middle East Insight* 5, no. 6 (1988): 30–35.

23. See for example the interview with Ariel Sharon, former minister of defense, in *Jerusalem Post International Edition*, August 20, 1988, p. 8.

24. See for example Alan Cowell, "Syria and Iran Assail New U.S.-P.L.O. Contacts," *New York Times*, December 17, 1988, p. 6.

25. For more on this aspect of the uprising see Robert Satloff, "Islam in the Palestinian Uprising," Policy Focus no. 7 (Washington: Washington Institute for Near East Policy, 1988).

26. This position is often based on United Nations General Assembly Resolution 181 of November 1947, which called for the creation of "independent Arab and Jewish states" and a "special international regime for the city of Jerusalem." The resolution defines an Israel considerably smaller than the one defined by the borders in force from 1948 to 1967. Yet even this partition was too much for the Arab states, which rejected the resolution and went to war with Israel as the British mandate ended in May 1948. The text of Resolution 181 is in Moore, *The Arab-Israeli Conflict*, 908–933.

27. See Harold H. Saunders, *The Other Walls: The Politics of the Arab-Israeli Peace Process* (Washington: American Enterprise Institute, 1985). For a similar set of suggestions see *Building For Peace: An American Strategy for the Middle East* (Washington: Washington Institute for Near East Policy, 1988).

28. The Reagan administration got it both wrong and right in 1988. Praise for Foreign Minister Shimon Peres, coupled with indirect criticism of his chief rival, Yitzhak Shamir, at a ceremony for Peres in May at

the White House was inappropriate and counterproductive, for it only strengthened those who were resisting the American policy of the time. Secretary of State Shultz did better in his public statements of what he saw as the cost of drift as his efforts of 1988 ran out of steam. See Robert Pear, "Shultz as Cassandra," *New York Times,* June 8, 1988, sec. A, pp. 1, 8.

29. For a similar view see Moshe Zak, "The Case against an International Conference on the Middle East," *Global Affairs,* no. 2 (Spring 1987): 34–50. For more positive assessments of the utility of an international conference and Soviet participation more generally see Nadav Safran, "Before the Storm," *New Republic,* December 12, 1988, pp. 16–17; Hermann F. Eilts, "Reviving the Middle East Peace Process: An International Conference?" *Middle East Insight* 5, no. 3 (1987); and *Toward Arab-Israeli Peace: Report of a Study Group* (Washington: Brookings Institution, 1988).

30. There would of course be arrangements governing the status of places holy to Muslims and Christians (and access to them).

31. Harold H. Saunders, "Reconstituting the Arab-Israeli Peace Process," in Quandt, *The Middle East,* 428.

32. See for example Ibrahim Abu-Lughod, "Imagine a Palestinian State," *New York Times,* April 25, 1988, sec. A, p. 21.

33. The text of the Palestinian National Charter of 1968 is in Moore, *The Arab-Israel Conflict,* 1085–91.

34. In May 1989 the Israeli government proposed an initiative for elections in the occupied territories. Key details of the initiative remain unresolved, and it is unclear whether the Palestinians will be willing to take part in the elections.

35. For more on what the United States might do in this area see Michael R. Gordon, "U.S. Urges Talks on Missiles in Mideast," *New York Times,* December 27, 1988, sec. A, p. 3.

## 3. GREECE, TURKEY, AND CYPRUS

1. For background on relations between Greece and Turkey and American relations with each see Jonathan Alford, ed., *Greece and Turkey: Adversity in Alliance* (New York: St. Martin's, 1984); Andrew Borowiec, *The Mediterranean Feud* (New York: Praeger, 1983); Theodore A. Couloumbis, *The United States, Greece, and Turkey: The Troubled Triangle* (New York: Praeger, 1983); and Kenneth Mackenzie, *Greece and Turkey: Disarray on NATO's Southern Flank* (London: Institute for the Study of Conflict, 1983).

2. For a full explanation of Aegean issues see Andrew Wilson, *The Aegean Dispute*, Adelphi Paper no. 155 (London: International Institute for Strategic Studies, 1979–80).

3. An unclassified version of NATO's proposal for resolving these jurisdictional disputes, put forward in 1980 by Gen. Bernard Rogers (Supreme allied commander, Europe) and normally referred to as the Rogers Plan, can be found in Robert McDonald, "Alliance Problems in the Eastern Mediterranean—Greece, Turkey and Cyprus: Part II," in *Prospects for Security in the Mediterranean* (London: International Institute for Strategic Studies, 1988), 87.

4. See Richard Haass, "Confidence-Building Measures and Naval Arms Control," in *The Future of Arms Control*, pt. 3, Confidence-Building Measures, ed. Jonathan Alford (London: International Institute for Strategic Studies, 1979), 23–29.

5. George Ball, *The Past Has Another Pattern: Memoirs* (New York: W. W. Norton, 1982), 350.

6. Henry A. Kissinger, *Years of Upheaval* (Boston: Little, Brown, 1982), 1191.

7. For the history of this episode see Nancy Crawshaw, *The Cyprus Revolt: An Account of the Struggle for Union with Greece* (Boston: George Allen and Unwin, 1978).

8. For a sense of how wide this gap can be see Christopher Hitchens, *Cyprus* (New York: Quartet, 1984); and R. R. Denktash, *The Cyprus Triangle* (Boston: George Allen and Unwin, 1982).

9. Brian Urquhart, *A Life in Peace and War* (New York: Harper and Row, 1987), 198.

10. For background to this meeting see Paul Lewis, "Greek and Turkish Cypriots to Resume Talks," *New York Times*, August 25, 1988, sec. A, p. 11; and "Well, They Met," *Economist*, August 27, 1988, p. 44.

11. See *Pravda*, January 22, 1986, p. 4; the complete text is reprinted in English in *Current Digest of the Soviet Press* 38, no. 3 (February 19, 1986): 16–17.


## 4. INDIA AND PAKISTAN

1. For background on the conflict and the American role see Dan Haendel, *The Process of Priority Formulation: U.S. Foreign Policy in the Indo-Pakistani War of 1971* (Boulder: Westview, 1977); S. S. Sethi, *The Decisive War: Emergence of a New Nation* (New Delhi: Sagan, 1972); and S. S. Bindra, *Indo-Pak Relations: Tashkent to the Simla Agreement* (New Delhi: Deep and Deep, 1981).

2. For background to the Simla accord and a copy of its text see Imtiaz H. Bokhari and Thomas Perry Thornton, *The 1972 Simla Agreement: An Asymmetrical Negotiation* (Washington: Johns Hopkins Foreign Policy Institute, 1988).

3. The beginning of the Soviet effort to improve relations with China can be traced to the address given by Gorbachev in the Pacific city of Vladivostok on July 28, 1986. For an analysis see Richard N. Haass, "The 'Europeanization' of Moscow's Asia Policy," *SAIS Review* 7, no. 2 (Summer–Fall 1987): 127–141.

4. An excellent statement summarizing the Reagan administration's approach to this part of the world is the address by Under Secretary of State Michael H. Armacost before the Asia Society, Washington, on April 29, 1987. The speech, "South Asia and the United States: An Evolving Partnership," is published by the Department of State as Current Policy no. 953.

5. The United States would not agree to supply nuclear fuel unless India accepted safeguards on all its nuclear facilities, including the Tarapur plant. India refused to accept such "full scope" safeguards, and the United States arranged for France to step in. This allowed India to get its fuel and the United States to abide by the letter of its policy if not by its spirit.

6. For a view of this problem from India see Conor Cruise O'Brien, "Holy War against India," *Atlantic Monthly*, August 1988, pp. 54–64.

7. For a more optimistic assessment of what can be accomplished in this area (including the possibility of getting India and Pakistan to sign a bilateral arms agreement that would establish a "balanced-imbalance" in India's favor that did not overly threaten Pakistan) see Stephen P. Cohen, "Security, Peace and Stability in South Asia: An American Perspective" (lecture presented to the University of Allahabad, India, February 20, 1987, published in 1987 by the Program in Arms Control, Disarmament, and International Security of the University of Illinois, Urbana-Champaign).

8. See Ben Barber, "India: Bully of the Orient?" *Washington Post*, January 1, 1989, sec. B, p. 5.

9. For some earlier background see Richard P. Cronin, "Prospects for Nuclear Proliferation in South Asia," *Middle East Journal* 37, no. 4 (Autumn 1983): 594–616.

10. For background see Rodney W. Jones, "Pakistan's Nuclear Options," in *Soviet-American Relations with Pakistan, Iran and Afghanistan*, ed. Hafeez Malik (New York: St. Martin's, 1987), 199–216.

11. For a summary of this flurry of statements and reactions see "A Pakistan Bombshell," *Newsweek*, March 16, 1987, p. 45.

12. A leading authority is Leonard Spector. See his *Nuclear Proliferation Today* (New York: Random House, 1984).

13. See the interview with President Zia ul-Haq of Pakistan in *Time*, March 30, 1987, p. 42.

14. The language (the Pressler amendment, with an annual certification that applies only to Pakistan) is required by Public Law 99-83, which in August 1985 amended Section 620 E of the Foreign Assistance Act. Section 620 E is the waiver provision that allows aid to go to a country that acquires unsafeguarded enrichment or reprocessing facilities; such aid is otherwise precluded under Section 669 of the same act.

15. In December 1987 Congress approved legislation providing Pakistan with $480 million in security assistance in fiscal year 1988, in the process waiving for thirty months provisions in the law that would have denied aid owing to Pakistani transgressions in the area of proliferation.

16. There is a rich literature on the likely impact of nuclear proliferation. An iconoclastic view that proliferation may be a stabilizing force is that of Kenneth N. Waltz, *The Spread of Nuclear Weapons: More May Be Better* (London: International Institute for Strategic Studies, 1971). A recent expression of Pakistani sentiments along these lines is Musahid Hussain, "Why Pakistan Needs a Nuclear Option," *Washington Post*, July 29, 1987. For the more traditional perspective see Albert Wohlstetter et al., *The Military Potential of Civilian Nuclear Energy: Moving Towards Life in a Nuclear Armed Crowd?* (Los Angeles: Pan Heuristics, 1975). Lewis A. Dunn and Herman Kahn, *Trends in Nuclear Proliferation, 1975–1995: Projections, Problems and Policy Options* (Croton-on-Hudson, N.Y.: Hudson Institute, 1976), provides a valuable survey of issues relating to managing proliferation (rather than preventing it).

17. "Pakistan and India Sign Pact," *Washington Post*, January 1, 1989, sec. A, pp. 31, 38. The agreement (unratified as of mid-1989) covers all nuclear-related facilities and provides that the two governments inform each other of the exact location of any such facilities.

18. See John H. Cushman Jr., "7 Nations Agree to Limit Export of Big Rockets," *New York Times*, April 17, 1987, sec. A, pp. 1, 6.

## 5. SOUTH AFRICA

1. For further discussion of Botha's reform efforts see *Race Relations Survey, 1985* (Johannesburg: South African Institute of Race Relations, 1986). This annual survey, published by an independent organization, provides extremely useful and detailed information on political, economic, social, and security-related developments in South Africa.

2. For a useful summary of the election and its implications see Pauline H. Baker, "South Africa: The Afrikaner Angst," *Foreign Policy* 69 (Winter 1987–88): 61–79.

3. There are 5,400 blacks and Coloureds serving full-time in the South African Army, which has a total full-time strength of 19,000. See *The Military Balance, 1988–1989* (London: International Institute for Strategic Studies, 1988), 140.

4. Leon Louw and Frances Kendall, *South Africa: The Solution* (Bisho, Ciskei: Amagi, 1986; San Francisco: Institute for Contemporary Studies, 1987, as *After Apartheid: The Solution for South Africa*). For a review of similar ideas see Arend Lijphart, *Power-Sharing in South Africa* (Berkeley: Institute of International Studies, University of California, 1985).

5. See "The South Africans Who Voted, and Those Who Stayed Away," *Economist*, October 29, 1988, pp. 43–44.

6. For insight into the challenges of implementing a reform strategy see two articles by Samuel P. Huntington: "Reform and Stability in South Africa," *International Security* 6, no. 4 (Spring 1982): 3–25; and "The Trouble With Reform," *Financial Mail*, October 24, 1986, pp. 85–87.

7. For the text of NSSM 39 see Mohamed A. El-Khawas and Barry Cohen, eds., *The Kissinger Study of Southern Africa: National Security Study Memorandum 39* (Westport, Conn.: Lawrence Hill, 1976).

8. For the text of Kissinger's speech see *Survival* 18, no. 4 (July–August 1976): 171–174.

9. For a short description of efforts during Carter's administration see Gaddis Smith, *Morality, Reason, and Power: American Diplomacy in the Carter Years* (New York: Hill and Wang, 1986), especially chapter 6.

10. Key aspects of what became the Reagan administration's policy were presented in an article written by Chester Crocker that appeared during the change in administrations from Carter to Reagan. See his "South Africa: Strategy for Change," *Foreign Affairs* 59, no. 2 (Winter 1980–81): 323–351. For a sense of the debate over Reagan's policy see Christopher Coker, *The United States and South Africa, 1968–1985: Constructive Engagement and Its Critics* (Durham: Duke University Press, 1986).

11. Shultz signaled the move away from constructive engagement and toward a more public line of opposition in a speech to the Business Council for International Understanding in New York on September 29, 1987. The text, entitled "The Democratic Future of South Africa," is published as Current Policy no. 1003 by the State Department's Bureau of Public Affairs.

12. See *Strategic Minerals: Extent of U.S. Reliance on South Africa* (Washington: U.S. General Accounting Office, 1988).

13. Karen Paul, "After the Americans Leave, What Then?" *New York Times*, August 7, 1988, sec. F, p. 3.

14. For a similar view see President Reagan's Report to the Congress of October 1987 pursuant to Section 501 of the Comprehensive Anti-Apartheid Act of 1986. For a dissenting view see Randall Robinson, "Turn Up Heat on Pretoria, *New York Times*, October 5, 1987, sec. A, p. 23; and John D. Battersby, "Sanctions Squeeze South Africa," *New York Times*, November 13, 1988, sec. F, pp. 1, 8. For a discussion of the mixed results of the decisions by five American companies to disinvest see *South Africa: Trends in Trade, Lending, and Investment* (Washington: U.S. General Accounting Office, 1988).

15. For example, recent statistics demonstrate that as the market shares of the United States and United Kingdom are dropping, those of West Germany and above all Japan are increasing. See *South Africa: Trends in Trade, Lending and Investment* (Washington: U.S. General Accounting Office, 1988), 10–21.

16. See for example David Roberts, Jr., "The ANC in Its Own Words," *Commentary*, July 1988, pp. 31–37.

17. For background see Leonard S. Spector, *Going Nuclear* (Cambridge, Mass.: Ballinger, 1987), 220–239; and Kurt M. Campbell and Michile A. Flournoy, "South Africa's Bomb: A Military Option?" *Orbis* 32, no. 3 (Summer 1988): 385–401.

18. *A U.S. Policy toward South Africa: The Report of the Secretary of State's Advisory Committee on South Africa* (Washington: U.S. Department of State, 1987), 3–4.

## 6. NORTHERN IRELAND

1. As is often the cases in emotional struggles of this sort, language and nomenclature have political overtones. The Catholics are often described as "nationalist," for they have a strong Catholic identity and wish to be associated (and integrated) with the Republic of Ireland. The Protestant majority was traditionally described as "unionist," for wanting to remain part of the United Kingdom rather than become independent or part of Ireland. Increasingly, however, the word "loyalist" is used to describe Protestant thinking, a shift that reflects increasing estrangement from London but continued, strong opposition to association with Dublin or significant power sharing with local Catholics. In addition, it should be noted none of the communities are mono-iths, and that these terms are necessarily generalizations that do not account for important distinctions and exceptions. For some general background to the dispute see John Darby, *Conflict in Northern Ire-*

*land* (London: Gill and Macmillan, 1976); Paul Arthur, *Government and Politics of Northern Ireland* (London: Longmans, 1980); and Patrick Buckland, *A History of Northern Ireland* (London: Gill and Macmillan, 1981).

2. For background to the Anglo-Irish accord and analysis of it see Malcolm Rutherford, "The Anglo-Irish Agreement," *World Today* 42, no. 1 (January 1986): 1–2; John F. McGarry and James E. Crimmins, "Stalemate in Northern Ireland?" *World Today* 43, no. 1 (January 1987): 8–11; Padraig O'Malley, "Ulster: The Marching Season," *Atlantic*, May 1986, pp. 28–34; William V. Shannon, "The Anglo-Irish Agreement," *Foreign Affairs* 64, no. 4, (1986): 849–870; and *Northern Ireland: An Anglo-Irish Dilemma?*, Conflict Studies No. 185 (London: Institute for the Study of Conflict, 1986). The last two items are also valuable overviews of the problem of Northern Ireland since the late 1960s.

3. For a similar critique of the Anglo-Irish accord see Andrew Sullivan, "War in Peace," *New Republic*, October 20, 1986, pp. 18–21.

4. For excellent surveys of the constitutional options see both David Watt, ed., *The Constitution of Northern Ireland: Problems and Prospects* (London: Heinemann, 1981), especially 183–214; and *Northern Ireland: Problems and Perspectives*, Conflict Studies no. 135, (London: Institute for the Study of Conflict, 1982), 39–43.

5. *Northern Ireland: Problems and Perspectives*, Conflict Studies no. 135 (London: Institute for the Study of Conflict, 1982), 38.

6. The IFI funds activities in such areas as tourism, urban development, business enterprise, agriculture and fisheries, and science and technology. There is a major focus on urban development. The United States provided $120 million for the period ending in 1988; Canada and New Zealand are providing much more modest financial support.

7. For useful insight into the security dilemma see "Brotherly Hate," *Economist*, June 25, 1988, pp. 19–22.

## 7. RIPENESS AND ITS IMPLICATIONS FOR POLICY

1. Henry Kissinger, *White House Years* (Boston: Little, Brown, 1979), 357.

2. David A. Lax and James K. Sebenius, *The Manager as Negotiator: Bargaining for Cooperation and Competitive Gain* (New York, Free Press, 1986), 59.

3. See for example John W. McDonald, Jr., and Diane B. Bendahmane, eds., *Conflict Resolution: Track Two Diplomacy* (Washington: Center for the Study of Foreign Affairs, Foreign Service Institute, U.S. Department of State, 1987).

# INDEX

Act of Union (1800), 123
Aegean Sea, 58, 59–64, 141, 142,
    149
Afghanistan, 12–14, 27, 28, 82,
    83, 84, 85, 90, 95, 142, 147
African National Congress (ANC),
    16, 102–04, 105, 106, 111, 113,
    116, 117–18, 119
Afrikaner Resistance Movement
    (AWB), 100, 111
Afrikaners, 110; political power
    of, 100, 111, 119, 121; rightward
    shift of, 101, 104, 105, 113, 115,
    140; indaba mistrusted by, 107;
    tribal basis of, 109; in bureauc-
    racy, 112
"Agni" missile, 92
Agreement on the Prevention of
    Dangerous Military Activities
    (1989), 64
Agreement on the Prevention of
    Incidents on and over the High
    Seas (1972), 63, 149
Airborne Warning and Control
    System (AWACS), 85–86
Ali Bhutto, Zulfikar, 82
Alliance party, 133
Allon, Yigal, 45
Amin, Hafizullah, 12
ANC. See African National

Congress
Anglo-Irish Agreement (1985),
    126, 128, 129, 131
Anglo-Irish War, 123
Angola, 11, 15–17, 114, 115, 116,
    144, 147
Annexation, of areas occupied by
    Israel, 32–33, 42–43, 51–52
Apartheid, 16, 99–100; alterna-
    tives to, 102–11; costs of, 121
Arafat, Yasir, 34, 35, 40, 41, 48
Arbitration, 28
Argentina: in Beagle Channel dis-
    pute, 9–10, 28; in Falklands
    war, 9–10, 19–21, 27, 28, 140
Arias, Oscar, 24
Assad, Hafez el-, 34
AWACS (Airborne Warning and
    Control System), 85–86
AWB (Afrikaner Resistance Move-
    ment), 100, 111

Ball, George, 65
Bangladesh, 80
Beagle Channel dispute, 9–10, 28,
    29
Begin, Menachem, 9, 28, 33, 144
"Benign neglect," 50, 88
Bern Agreement (1976), 62
Bhutto, Benazir, 91, 94